PENGUIN BOOKS

Selected Poems: Brian Patten

Brian Patten was born in Liverpool in 1946. His work first appeared in the bestselling Penguin collection *The Mersey Sound* in 1967 (with Roger McGough and the late Adrian Henri). Among his individual collections are *Little Johnny's Confession*; *Notes to the Hurrying Man*; *The Irrelevant Song*; *Vanishing Trick*; *Grave Gossip* and *Armada*. He is the editor of *The Puffin Book of Modern Children's Verse* and his poetry for children includes the highly popular collections *Gargling With Jelly*; *Thawing Frozen Frogs*; and *Juggling With Gerbils*. He has won numerous awards, including the Cholmondeley Award for Poetry, and a special award from the Mystery Writers of America Guild for his children's novel, *Mr Moon's Last Case*. He is a Fellow of the Royal Society of Literature. In 2002 he was honoured with the Freedom of the City of Liverpool.

Selected Poems

BRIAN PATTEN

PENGUIN BOOKS

PENGUIN BOOKS

Published by the Penguin Group
Penguin Books Ltd, 80 Strand, London WC2R 0RL, England
Penguin Group (USA) Inc., 375 Hudson Street, New York, New York 10014, USA
Penguin Group (Canada), 90 Eglinton Avenue East, Suite 700, Toronto, Ontario, Canada M4P 2Y3
(a division of Pearson Penguin Canada Inc.)
Penguin Ireland, 25 St Stephen's Green, Dublin 2, Ireland (a division of Penguin Books Ltd)
Penguin Group (Australia), 250 Camberwell Road, Camberwell, Victoria 3124, Australia
(a division of Pearson Australia Group Pty Ltd)
Penguin Books India Pvt Ltd, 11 Community Centre, Panchsheel Park, New Delhi – 110 017, India
Penguin Group (NZ), 67 Apollo Drive, Mairangi Bay, Auckland 1310, New Zealand
(a division of Pearson New Zealand Ltd)
Penguin Books (South Africa) (Pty) Ltd, 24 Sturdee Avenue, Rosebank, Johannesburg 2196, South Africa

Penguin Books Ltd, Registered Offices: 80 Strand, London WC2R 0RL, England

www.penguin.com

First published in Penguin Books 2007
1

Set in Monotype Sabon
Typeset by Rowland Phototypesetting Ltd, Bury St Edmunds, Suffolk
Printed in England by Clays Ltd, St Ives plc

ISBN: 978-0-141-02713-5

For Linda

Contents

Author's Note

The earliest of these poems, 'Sleep Now', was written when I was fifteen, the latest when I was sixty. Except for a couple of strays which I felt belonged, emotionally at least, elsewhere in the selection, the poems are presented in a rough chronological order. I have also included a dozen new poems as well as several from my books for children. Because they are available in a separate collection elsewhere, I have drawn less from my love poems for this selection than I otherwise might have done.

The Projectionist's Nightmare

This is the projectionist's nightmare:
A bird finds its way into the cinema,
Finds the beam, flies down it,
Smashes into a screen depicting a garden,
A sunset and two people being nice to each other.
Real blood, real intestines, slither down
  the likeness of a tree.
'This is no good,' screams the audience,
'This is not what we came to see.'

Where Are You Now, Batman?

Where are you now, Batman? Now that Aunt Heriot has
  reported Robin missing
And Superman's fallen asleep in the sixpenny childhood
  seats?
Where are you now that Captain Marvel's SHAZAM! echoes
  round the auditorium?
The magicians don't hear, must all be deaf . . . or dead.
The Purple Monster who came down from The Purple
  Planet disguised as a man
Is wandering aimlessly about the streets
With no way of getting back;
Sir Galahad's been strangled by the Incredible Living Trees,
Zorro killed by his own sword.
In the junk-ridden, disused hangars
Blackhawk's buried the last of his companions;
Rocket Man's fuel tanks have given out over London.
Though the Monster and the Ape still fight it out
In a room where the walls are continually closing
No one is watching.
Even Flash Gordon's been abandoned,
A star-wanderer weeping over robots loved
        half a universe ago.

My celluloid companions, it's only a few years
Since I first knew you, yet already something in us has
  faded.
Did we kill you off simply by growing up?
We who made you possible with our unsophisticated minds
And with our pocket money
And the sixpences we received for pretending to be good?

Sucked from tiny terraces on Saturday mornings
We cheered you on from disaster to disaster,
Never imagining how that Terrible Fiend,
        that Ghastly Adversary
Mr Old Age, would catch you in his deadly trap
And come finally to polish you off,
His machine gun dripping with years.

Sleep now

In memory of Wilfred Owen

Sleep now,
Your blood moving in the quiet wind;
No longer afraid of the rabbits
Hurrying through the tall grass
Or the faces laughing from
The beach and among cold trees.

Sleep now,
Alone in the sleeves of grief,
Listening to clothes falling
And your flesh touching God;
To the chatter and backslapping
Of Christ meeting heroes of war.

Sleep now,
Your words have passed
The lights shining from the East
And the sound of flak
Raping graves and emptying seasons.

You do not hear the dry wind pray
Or the children play a game called soldiers
In the street.

Little Johnny's Confession

This morning
    being rather young and foolish
    I borrowed a machine gun my father
    had left hidden since the war, went out,
    and eliminated a number of small enemies
    Since then I have not returned home.

This morning
    swarms of police with tracker dogs
    wander about the city
    with my description printed
    on their minds, asking:
    'Have you seen him?
    He is seven years old,
    likes Pluto, Mighty Mouse
    and Biffo the Bear,
    have you seen him, anywhere?'

This morning
    sitting alone in a strange playground
    muttering you've blundered, you've blundered
    over and over to myself
    I work out my next move
    but cannot move.
    The tracker dogs will sniff me out,
    they have my lollypops.

Come into the City, Maud

'Come into the garden, Maud,
For the black bat, night, has flown.'
– Tennyson

Maud, where are you, Maud?
With your long dresses and peachcream complexion;
In what cage did you hang that black bat night?
What took place in the garden? Maud, it is over,
You can tell us now.

Still lyrical but much used, you wander about the suburbs
Watching the buses go past full of young happy people,
Wondering where the garden is, wherever can it be,
And how can it be lost. Maud, it's no use.

Can it be that you got yourself lost
And are living with an out-of-work musician,
You share a furnished room and have an old wireless
That tells you the latest bad news.
What's happening, Maud?

Do you wear a Mary Quant dress
And eat fish and chips alone at night?
Wear make-up that tastes of forget-me-nots?
Where are you? and are you very lost,
Very much alone?
Do you cry for that garden, lost among pornographic
suggestions,
Where the concrete flowers neither open nor close;
Who poured weedkiller over your innocence?

Maud, it's much later now.
Between the concrete banks the rivers of the sky run,
Black estuaries polluted by stars.
And daily beneath them
We wound ourselves,
Ignorant of any tenderness we hide in each other's lives
A clue to our loneliness.

We could not find that garden for you,
Even if we tried.
So, come into the city, Maud,
Where flowers are too quickly picked
And the days are butchered as if they were enemies.

Maud, is that you I see
Alone among the office blocks,
Head bowed, young tears singing pop-sorrow
On your cheeks?

Johnny Learns the Language

Yesterday
in order to explain myself
I locked myself away
with an old alphabet,
with the hand-me-down phrases for which
I had no use but to which
I was already addicted.

Yesterday,
while considering how absurd it was
that everything has a name
I discovered that the mayfly
was weighed down by a single vowel.
Under the threat of not being understood
I began to understand
how words were the nets in which
what I was floundered.

Mother,
you come with your bowl of words,
fat words, puffed with kindness.
And father
you come with your silences in which
words sneak about like thieves.

I am learning your language.
'Loss' 'Defeat' 'Regret' –
without understanding
you would have these be
the blueprints for my future.

Little Johnny's Night Visitor

Last night,
before sleep ambushed me,
the bogeyman came.
He limped up the stairs,
stood on the landing,
whispered my name.

I pretended not to hear him.
I conjured up some heroes.
I was invisible.
I was bulletproof.
I could fly away from him,
leap out the window, leap
across the rooftops to escape him.

Last night
I heard him try the door of my bedroom.
I heard him cross the room.
I locked the sheets,
I made the bed into iron.
I made myself so tiny he could not find me.

Last night,
before sleep could rescue me,
the bogeyman came.
Drunk, he stumbled over words
he will never repeat again.

Father,
please do not stare at me.
Do not come so close.
I do not know how to love strangers.

Winter Note

It's evening and the streets are cold again.
The cars go past in such a hurry you'd think
The world full of emergencies.
The young men and women no longer parading
Hurry from the supermarkets,
Feigning a lack of caring, their tins
Glow with loneliness.
Leaves gone, scents gossip of previous winters.

And what did we do then?
Were the florists' windows stuffed with bright icy flowers?
Were the sirens as persistent, the parks as barren?
Whose hand was held, whose face
Did we swear never to forget?

As always the rooms are damp, the furniture ancient.
Yet among this drabness is a light, self-created.
The wine stains on the carpet emerge as roses,
The fridge becomes a grotto.
We fill our heads with dreams still.
In this season we are all that blossoms.

A Creature to Tell the Time by

I created for myself
a creature to tell the time by
– and on the lawns of her tongue
flowers grew,
sweet scented words fell
out her mouth, her eyes and paws were comforting –
and woken with her
at dawn, with living birds

humming, alien
inside my head,

I sensed inside us both
the green love that grew there yesterday
was dead.

Little Johnny's Final Letter

Mother,
I won't be home this evening, so
don't worry; don't hurry to report me missing.
Don't drain the canals to find me,
I've decided to stay alive, don't
search the woods, I'm not hiding,
simply gone to get myself classified.
Don't leave my Shreddies out,
I've done with security.
Don't circulate my photograph to society,
I have disguised myself as a man
and am giving priority to obscurity.
It suits me fine;
I have taken off my short trousers
and put on long ones, and
now am going out into the city, so
don't worry; don't hurry to report me missing.

I've rented a room without any curtains
and sit behind the windows growing cold;
heard your plea on the radio this morning,
you sounded sad and strangely old.

Portrait of a Young Girl Raped at a Suburban Party

And after this quick bash in the dark
You will rise and go
Thinking of how empty you have grown
And of whether all the evening's care in front of mirrors
And the younger boys disowned
Led simply to this.

Confined to what you are expected to be
By what you are,
Out in this frozen garden
You shiver and vomit –
Frightened, drunk among trees,
You wonder at how those acts that called for tenderness
Were far from tender.

Now you have left your titterings about love
And your childishness behind you
Yet still far from being old
You spew up among flowers
And in the warm stale rooms
The party continues.

It seems you saw some use in moving away
from that group of drunken lives
Yet already ten minutes pregnant
In twenty thousand you might remember
This party
This dull Saturday evening
When planets rolled out of your eyes
And splashed down in suburban gardens.

Prose Poem towards a Definition of Itself

When in public poetry should take off its clothes and wave to the nearest person in sight; it should be seen in the company of thieves and lovers rather than that of journalists and publishers. On sighting mathematicians it should unhook the algebra from their minds and replace it with poetry; on sighting poets it should unhook poetry from their minds and replace it with algebra; it should fall in love with children and woo them with fairy tales; it should wait on the landing for two years for its mates to come home then go outside and find them all dead.

When the electricity fails it should wear dark glasses and pretend to be blind. It should guide all those who are safe into the middle of busy roads and leave them there. It should shout EVIL! EVIL! from the roofs of the world's stock exchanges. It should not pretend to be a clerk or a librarian. It is the eventual sameness of contradictions. It should never weep until it is alone and then only after it has covered the mirrors and sealed up the cracks.

Poetry should seek out couples and wander with them into stables, neglected bedrooms and engineless cars for a final Good Time. It should enter burning factories too late to save anyone. It should pay no attention to its real name.

Poetry should be seen lying by the side of road accidents, be heard hissing from unlit gas rings. It should scrawl the teacher's secret on a blackboard, offer her a worm saying, Inside this is a tiny apple.

Poetry should play hopscotch in the 6 p.m. streets and look for jinks in other people's dustbins. At dawn it should leave the bedroom and catch the first bus home. It should be seen standing on the ledge of a skyscraper, on a bridge with a brick tied around its heart. It is the monster hiding in a child's dark room, it is the scar on a beautiful man's face. It is the last blade of grass being picked from the city park.

Note to the Hurrying Man

All day I sit here doing nothing but
watching how at daybreak
birds fly out and return no fatter
when it's over. Yet hurrying about this room
you would have me do something similar;
would have me make myself a place
in that sad traffic you call a world.
Don't hurry me into it; offer
no excuses, no apologies.
Until their brains snap open
I have no love for those who rush
about its mad business;
put their children on a starting line and push
into Christ knows what madness.

You will not listen.
'Work at life!' you scream,
and working I see you rushing everywhere,
so fast most times you ignore
two quarters of your half a world.
If all slow things are useless,
take no active part in nor justify your ignorance
that's fine; but why bother screaming after me?
Afraid perhaps to come to where I've stopped
in case you find
into some slow and glowing countryside
yourself escaping.
Screams measure and keep up the distance between us:
Be quieter –
I really do need to escape;
map out the route you might take
If ever this hurrying is over.

The Pint-sized Ark

William stood in the encroaching dark
Banging nails into a pint-sized Ark.
People gathered round and they mocked
Each single nail mad William knocked
Into the Ark, the pint-sized Ark,
Standing in the encroaching dark
Between the tower-block and park.

William, banging, what's it for?
Don't you know it's been done before?

A policeman came, and he made a note:
'It's hardly the size of a rowing boat,
The Ark's so small he will hardly get
Himself in along with the family pet.'

True, thought William, but my soul will fit,
And that's all need go into it.

BANG BANG drip BANG BANG drip
BANG drip BANG BANG drip BANG drip

His face was vacant, in his eye was a spark,
And his hammer beat in time to the encroaching dark.

The Beast

Something that was not there before
has come through the mirror
into my room.

It is not such a simple creature
as first I thought –
from somewhere it has brought a mischief

that troubles both silence and objects,
and now left alone here
I weave intricate reasons for its arrival.

They disintegrate. Today, in January, with
the light frozen on my window, I hear outside
a million panicking birds, and know even out there

comfort is done with; it has shattered
even the stars, this creature
at last come home to me.

Ode on Celestial Music

(or, It's The Girl in the Bathroom Singing)

It's not celestial music,
it's the girl downstairs in the bathroom singing.
You can tell. Although it's winter
the trees outside her window have grown leaves,
all manner of flowers push up through the floorboards.
I think – what a filthy trick that is to play on me,
I snip them with my scissors shouting
'I want only bona fide celestial music!'
Hearing this she stops singing.

Out of her bath now the girl knocks on my door.
'Is my singing disturbing you?' she smiles entering.
'Did you say it was licentious or sensual?
And excuse me, my bath towel's slipping.'
A warm and blonde creature.
I slam the door on her breasts shouting
'I want only bona fide celestial music!'

Much later on in life I wear my hearing aid.
What have I done to my body, ignoring it,
splitting things into so many pieces my hands
cannot mend anything? The stars, the buggers, remained
silent.
Down in the bathroom now her daughter is singing.
Turning my hearing aid full volume
I bend close to the floorboards hoping
for at least one song to get through.

Interruption at the Opera House

At the very beginning of an important symphony,
while the rich and famous were settling into their quietly
expensive boxes,

a man came crashing through the crowds,
carrying in his hand a cage in which
the rightful owner of the music sat,
yellow and tiny and very poor;
and taking onto the rostrum this rather timid bird
he turned up the microphones, and it sang.

'A very original beginning to the evening,' said the crowds,
quietly glancing at their programmes to find
the significance of the intrusion.

Meanwhile at the box office, the organizers of the evening
were arranging for small and uniformed attendants
to evict, even forcefully, the intruders.
But as the attendants, poor and gathered from the nearby
slums at little expense,
went rushing down the aisles to do their job
they heard, above the coughing and irritable rattle of
jewels,
a sound that filled their heads with light,
and from somewhere inside them there bubbled up a
stream,
and there came a breeze on which their youth was carried.
How sweetly the bird sang!

And though soon the fur-wrapped crowds
were leaving their boxes and in confusion were winding
their way home
still the attendants sat in the aisles,
and some, so delighted at what they heard, rushed out to
call
their families and friends.

And their children came,
sleepy for it was late in the evening,
very late in the evening,
and they hardly knew if they had done with dreaming
or had begun again.

In all the tenement blocks
the lights were clicking on,
and the rightful owner of the music,
tiny but no longer timid, sang
for the rightful owners of the song.

If You Had to Hazard a Guess Who Would You Say Your Poetry Is for?

For people who have nowhere to go in the afternoons,
For people who the evening banishes to small rooms,
For good people, people huge as the world.
For people who give themselves away forgetting
What it is they are giving,
And who are never reminded.
For people who cannot help being kind
To the hand bunched in pain against them.
For inarticulate people,
People who invent their own ugliness,
Who invent pain, terrified of blankness;
And for people who stand forever at the same junction
Waiting for the chances that have passed.
And for those who lie in ambush for themselves,
Who invent toughness as a kind of disguise,
Who, lost in their narrow and self-defeating worlds,
Carry remorse inside them like a plague;
And for the self-seeking self lost among them
I hazard a poem.

The Obsolete Nightingale

When long ago it became apparent that the lion
had no intentions of lying down with the lamb
you, still believing in that obsolete fable,
were thrown into chaos.

From somewhere inside you
time and again you dragged out the lamb,
and inviting the lion in from the nervous world
put the fable to the test.

Each night through the walls the slaughter leaked,
your neighbours became addicted.

A terminal romantic, a confused source-seeker,
in the bedrooms of cheap hotels you open your suitcase,
and unfolding the soiled rainbows
sleep among them.

*

Poetry is the interval during which nothing is said,
the sign-board on which nothing is written.
It is the astronaut stepping for the first time into liquid
space.
It follows its imagination out across the frozen lakes,
out to where the small footprints have ended.

It is the surgeon cutting deeper and deeper,
bewildered by the depths.
It sings for the children who keep clouds in their pockets,
for the midwives tasting of grass,
for the impending dust,

for the card-dealers who pull out the Milky Way
as a last resort.

At the festival of fools it erects a bedraggled maypole
and dances to a music of its own invention.

In the conference rooms where the great minds gather
where the politicians squark
and the philosophers brood
it serves the drinks,
in the halls where the fashionable dance
it robs the overcoats.

It stands in red kiosks exhausting
the phone books of generations.
It is the silence in a time
of acceptable lies.

*

When the professor of literature steps into the shadow of a
  lectern
and when the students are finally seated
and the whispers have died away
poetry puts on an overcoat
and sick of threadbare souls,
steps out into the streets weeping.

It is the clue overlooked by policemen;
the stranger walking through the airport terminal;
the blue egg found crushed in a nest.

It is the address thrown from the window
of a passing train.

*

I sit in motorway cafés staring through windows.
You are there,
running across the wet fields,
the logicians howling after you.

They have given the hounds platefuls of roses,
stuffed their noses with tulips –
they'll give you no rest, poetry.
From the roofs of articulate houses
the scholars will snipe at you.

It is rumoured one among them
has transmuted gold into dust.

I have found you among strangers,
among faces that pick about in time,
choosing the length of their days
and the length of their suffering.

*

I have found you most often in sadness,
on evenings when each patch of ground
seems remote as an island,
when rooms are bleakest and speech is incoherent,
when words choke,
fish thrown up from the paranoiac pools.

You belong to these generations drifting between buildings,
unlovely mammals, pale as worms,
lamenting their own temporariness.
You are the chameleon crawling across rainbows.

I am anchored among your contradictions:
wrapped in obsolete kindness,
too caring in days ruled by slaughter,

too gentle among the truncheons and the nights fed on
disaster
you wander about the city whispering
'Where's the bloodbath this evening?'
'What new mutilations are available?'
You wander through each face looking for the one
that will best mirror your own.
The list of your affairs is endless.

*

Poetry asks the head office for its files on the nightingale,
for all information regarding its colour,
its shape, the kind of song it indulged in.
The message comes back:
'Subject obsolete. File closed.'

6.15 a.m.
Across the Thames busloads of charladies wander
gossiping about disease;
truckloads of bleached meat unloaded in front of futuristic
towers.
Worn faces, faded print dresses,
exhausted overcoats,
all refusing to announce the daylight as miracle.
Poetry, you were born among them.

The Embankment is thick with rain,
with cardboard boxes in which dignity flounders.
From the river poetry fishes out an image
of a dead bird floating beneath vanished starlight.

It is the same old story.
Night owns the copyright.

And always there will be the dream of travelling,
of boarding the boats sailing from trivia,
And always there will be the regret,
the sense of carnivals finished.

*

Poetry, what of your education? Early on you learned to loathe the literati's clever games – those spiels for the intellect that left untouched people stuck in the rut down which most human longings flow. Your vocabulary was limited, you studied impossibilities, wrote essays on impatience that were never finished, you stared at the atlas, invented journeys you were too young to set out upon. You planned meetings with alien invaders. In the school laboratories you invented a cure for obedience.

Were you hidden, disguised as frost on the spiky railings of schoolyards? Did you sneak into the classroom and settle, quiet as dust, onto the shoulders of restless children? Time and again I have gone to you for advice and searching through pages of unremarkable confessions have found among the heart's trash nothing but revelations. You are the mirror in front of which the years tremble. You are the laughter borrowed momentarily from strangers. You are the final sentence, echoing forever.

After Frost

It's hard to tell what bird it is
Singing in the misty wood,
Or the reason for its song
So late after evening's come.

When all else has dropped its name
Down into the scented dark
Its song grown cool and clear says
Nothing much to anyone,

But catches hold a whisper in my brain
That only now is understood.
It says, rest your life against this song,
It's rest enough for anyone.

A Talk with a Wood

Moving through you one evening
when you offered shelter to
quiet things soaked in rain

I saw through your thinning branches
the beginnings of suburbs, and
frightened by the rain,

grey hares running upright in
distant fields, and quite alone there
thought of nothing but my footprints

being filled, and love, distilled
of people, drifted free, and then
the wood spoke to me.

Travelling between Places

Leaving nothing and nothing ahead;
when you stop for the evening
the sky will be in ruins.

When you hear late birds
with tired throats singing
think how good it is that they,

knowing you were coming,
stayed up late to greet you,
who travel between places

when the late afternoon
drifts into the woods, when
nothing matters specially.

Frogs in the Wood

How good it would be to be lost again,
Night falling on the compass and the map
Turning to improbable flames,
Bright ashes going out in the ponds.

And how good it would be
To stand bewildered in a strange wood
Where you are the loudest thing,
Your heart making a deafening noise.

And how strange when your fear of being lost has subsided
To stand listening to the frogs holding
Their arguments in the streams,
Condemning the barbarous herons.

And how right it is
To shrug off real and invented grief
As of no importance
To this moment of your life,

When being lost seems
So much more like being found,
And you find all that is lost
Is what weighed you down.

The Shadow-puppet's Complaint

Not quite drunk yet, I lean across the table
And gossip with my shadow.
We have intimate conversations
About the day's non-events,
About where they are leading and
The brightness they have fled from.
It smiles at my attempts to give substance
To that skeleton, Memory.

My shadow munches on the shadow of an apple,
And does not fill me.

I listen in horror as it complains
Of the raw edge gone from love,
And though I wish to fault all it says
My arguments are insubstantial.
It has an army of confederates to back
Every claim it can make against me.

Like a shabby magician
It conjures up the past,
Parades before me
All my mistakes,
My indiscretions.
It has drawn into itself
Everything for which I hungered.

Even in darkness I cannot escape it:
At night I dream of a stream that flows
Undauntingly through all things,
That clears away longings so old
They have festered.
My shadow sits beside it, thirsting.

Recently an avalanche of deaths
Has softened its tongue.
It asks questions of me
So simple they can hardly be answered.
When did you last weep?
Was there a witness?

It has begun to speak of what is still felt
For a friend not seen these last few years.
It can no longer remember which of us
Loved her best,
Nor even if that love was real,
Or a shadow.

I remember once how after she had gone
I sat like this in a different room.
I think it was only my shadow that wept,
And went out into the night in search of her.

Song for Last Year's Wife

Alice, this is my first winter
of waking without you, of knowing
that you, dressed in familiar clothes,
are elsewhere, perhaps not even
conscious of our anniversary. Have
you noticed? The earth's still as hard,
the same empty gardens exist? It is
as if nothing special had changed.
I wake with another mouth feeding
from me, but still feel as if
love had not the right
to walk out of me. A year now. So
what? you say. I send out my spies
to find who you are living with, what
you are doing. They return, smile
and tell me your body's as firm,
you are as alive, as warm and inviting
as when they knew you first.
   Perhaps it is the winter,
its isolation from other seasons, that
sends me your ghost to witness
when I wake. Somebody came here today, asked
how you were keeping, what you were doing.
I imagine you, waking in another city,
enclosed by this same hour. So
ordinary a thing as loss comes now
and touches me.

Ripe for Conversion

The God-freaks, their bibles
Burning with improbable flames,
Have singled me out again.
Perhaps they see in me a pit
Only God can fill. Their thrill
Is to catch me on street corners
Or coming out of bars where their quarry,
The proletariat, gather.
Like salesmen whose patter devalues
The goods they are selling, they
Reduce Heaven and its prophets
To a crutch and a cliché.
They're like morose cenobites
Whose isolation is secular and spreads
From room to room, and is malignant.
Watching them forage so earnestly
Among the crowd they cannot encompass,
Sometimes out of charity I let
Their soul-squad catch me,
Listen to them talk until
They spill out their own history.
Yet it makes me uneasy the way
They see in me someone
Not so different from themselves;
A man exiled from himself,
In a state of mild decay, like a house
No one lives in any more,
Ripe for conversion.

Albatross Ramble

I woke this morning to find an albatross staring at me.
Funny, it wasn't there last night.
Last night I was alone.

The albatross lay on the bed.
The sheets were soaking.

I live miles from any coast.
I invited no mad sailors home.
I dreamt of no oceans.

The bird watches me carefully.
I watch it carefully.
For some particular reason I think
Maybe we deserve one another.

It's sunny outside, spring even.
The sky is bright; it is alive.

I remember I have someone to meet,
Someone clear, someone with whom I'm calm,
Someone who lets things glow.

As I put on my coat to go out
I think that maybe after all
I don't deserve this bird.

Albatrosses cause hang-ups.
There's not much I can do with them.
I can't give them in to zoos.
The attendants have enough albatrosses.

Nobody is particularly eager to take it from me.
I think, Maybe the bird's in the wrong house.
Maybe it meant to go next door.
Maybe some sailor lives next door.
Maybe it belongs to the man upstairs.
Maybe it belongs to the girls in the basement.
It must belong to someone.

I rush into the corridor and shout:
'Does anyone own an albatross? Has anyone lost it?
There's an albatross in my room!'

I'm met by an awkward silence.

I know the man upstairs is not happy.
I know the girls in the basement wander lost among the
furniture.
Maybe they're trying to get rid of it
And won't own up.
Maybe they've palmed the albatross off on me.

I don't want an albatross; I don't want this bird.
I've got someone to meet,
Someone patient, someone good and healthy,
Someone whose hands are warm and whose grin
Makes everything babble and say yes.
I'd not like my friend to meet the albatross.

It would eat those smiles;
It would bother that patience;
It would peck at those hands
Till they turned sour and ancient.

Although I have made albatross traps,
Although I have sprayed the thing with glue,
Although I have fed it every poison available,

It persists in living,
This bird with peculiar shadows
Casts its darkness over everything.

If I go out it would only follow me.
It would flop in the seat next to me on the bus,
Scowling at the passengers.
If I took it to the park it would only bother the ducks,
Haunt couples in rowing boats,
Tell the trees it's winter.
It would be patted by policemen as they gently asked:
'Have you an albatross licence?'

Gloom bird, doom bird,
I can do nothing about it.
There are no albatross-exterminators in the directory,
I looked for hours.

Maybe it will stay with me right through summer;
Maybe it has no intentions of leaving.
I'll grow disturbed with this bird never leaving,
This alien bird with me all the time.

And now my friend is knocking on the door,
Less patient, frowning,
A bit sad and angry.

I'll sit behind this door and make noises like an albatross.
A terrible crying.
I'll put my mouth to the keyhole and wail albatross wails.
My friend will know then
I have an albatross in my room.
My friend will sympathize with me,
Go away knowing it's not my fault I can't open the door.

I'll wait here; I might devise some plan:
It's spring and everything is good but for this.
This morning I woke with an albatross in my room.
There's nothing much I can do about it until it goes away.

Bottle-talk

When you have turned away
From the crowds and the bars
That first shaped then owned you
Don't convince yourself
It was they that harmed you.
Isolation disfigures men
Who think their separateness superior.
It was not fulfilling
The things you longed for
First shamed you;
Each day belittled
By the night's
Drunken exultations.
And each dawn the same
Comic opera re-enacted:
Sober and cautious you watch
As all your resolutions faded
Back into dream-status.
Those intentions were merely bottle-talk,
Inconsistent ambitions
Dull days ignited.
There is only this certainty –
By the bottle's dull genie
None of your wishes
Will ever be granted.

The Want

Where do longings go
When we let them go
And say we do not care?

They do not vanish into air,
But mingling with the blood
Create a poison there.

And where now the want,
The ache without a wound
That beat slow time in the heart's
Once new-found core?

Relinquished,
Abandoned, all
That was raw?

Salvage Operation

Those parts of myself I let escape, where did they go?
Those marauding bands of sentiment that crossed
The heart's hardening frontier?
Where did they end up,
Those qualities thrown aside and now sought again,
So late on, and in such earnest?
All those strands of the self that fled as the soul corroded,
They must have sought refuge, but where?
Believing they can be nowhere other than inside me
Almost nightly now I search for them,
But trawling through physical paranoia
Find little but fragments to remind me
Of the bright days wasted.
Yet because beginning over again
Is a fairy tale the grave denies us,
And because there is still much gathering in to be done,
Many repatriations to be attempted,
I tell myself, *Dive again, dreamer,*
Back down into the currents of the mutable self
Where much of what was lost might still drift,
Battered, but salvageable.

Nursery Rhyme for the Sleepless

Suckablood, Suckablood, where have you been?'
'I've been in the brain of a Dreaming Machine.'

'Suckablood, Suckablood, what did you there?'
'I taught it of sorrow and loss, pain and despair.'

'Suckablood, Suckablood, were the lessons much fun?'
'I spoke sombrely of all that is soon come and soon gone.'

'Suckablood, Suckablood, does it know what you've
done!?'
'I think it has some inkling of what has begun.'

'If it wants no more lessons, then what's to be done?'
'Don't worry, to me I am sure it will come.'

'Suckablood, Suckablood, what if it's late?'
'Then in the grave my lessons will keep.'

Night Piece

All day I have spent building this web,
This necessary extension strung between
Objects unfamiliar and uncertain.
Over those things to which it is anchored
I have no power. My trust must be explicit.
So far I have caught rain, sunlight,
Particles of leaf, and things so small
They cannot satisfy.
At night in a crack between concrete
I dream of catching something so immense
It would shake the web's centre;
Awkward and meat-ridden, its wings
Would snap and dullen my creation.
Of such an event I am terrified,
For such an event I am longing.

You Come to Me Quiet as Rain Not Yet Fallen

You come to me quiet as rain not yet fallen
afraid of how you might fail yourself your
dress seven summers old is kept open
in memory of sex, smells warm, of boys,
and of the once long grass.
But we are colder now; we have not
love's first magic here. You come to me
quiet as bulbs not yet broken
out into sunlight.

The fear I see in your now lining face
changes to puzzlement when my hands reach
for you as branches reach. Your dress
does not fall easily, nor does your body
sing of its own accord. What love added to
a common shape no longer seems a miracle.
You come to me with your age wrapped in excuses
and afraid of its silence.

Into the paradise our younger lives made
of this bed and room
has leaked the world and all its questioning,
and now those shapes terrify us most
that remind us of our own. Easier now
to check longings and sentiment,
to pretend not to care overmuch,
you look out across the years, and you come to me
quiet as the last of our senses closing.

Friends

For Liz Kylle and Harry Fainlight

I met them in bars and in railway stations
And I met them in borrowed rooms and at bright
  gatherings,
And often enough
I met them with misgivings and doubts,
And misinterpreted what they said
Or did not understand at all, or understood so well
No explanations seemed needed.
And still, for all this, I kept on losing them.

Changes took place, and things that had seemed
Extraordinary and out of reach
Became life's most obvious gifts,
And the world slowed down and I began
To meet them less and less.

Then I learned how the exodus from this place
Is not scheduled,
At times the young leave before the old
And the old
Are left gaping at their fortune.

And now, Harry, you too are caught in your own
'*Miraculous stream that flows uphill*',
Caught up in its flow towards Heaven,
And flesh has dropped away from Love
And bald, bleak memory is all we hold of you.

Looking through an address book containing
The names they have abandoned
I realize that as from today
I haven't fingers enough to count
The graves in which they are exiled.

Turning the Pages

Late at night I sat turning the pages
Half-looking for the lines I'd once read,
Astonished at their simplicity.
Late at night I sat turning the pages,
My tongue uprooting miniature lights, infatuated
By what it hoped to become.
I sat turning the pages ignoring
The voices asking,
'What answers can be found
By simply turning the pages?'
While the future amassed its griefs
And things left undone squabbled and multiplied
I sat turning the pages,
And slowly I learned
How to abandon the future
And leave it less crowded,
And I began to understand
How there is nothing complicated in this world
That is not of my own making,
And how for years I had lived
Under the scrutiny of the blind,
Believing they could see me best.
Lacking confidence not in what I was
But in what others considered me
I almost became what they considered me.
Now I am glad I lacked such confidence,
And sat late at night turning the pages,
Turning the pages ignoring
The voices asking
What answers can be found

By simply turning the pages,
Late at night turning the pages
Half-looking for the lines you once read,
Astonished at their simplicity.

Early in the Evening

I met her early in the evening
The cars were going home
I was twenty-four and dreaming
My head was full of shadows her brightness cancelled
Beneath her dress her breasts were pushing
It was early in the evening
Spring was only a few streets away
In the closed parks the leaves were trying
The pubs had nothing to give us
Early in the evening
When the street railings were burning
There was nothing much to do but to be together

She drifted into sleep early in the evening
Her head was on the pillow
The sun that fell about her
Drifted in the window
Early in the evening
Some birds still sang on rooftops
Their hearts could have fitted into egg cups
It was early in the evening
The sky was going purple
Her dress lay on a chair by the window
Early in the evening she had shook it from her
She was awake and she was dreaming
Her head was free of shadows
Her belly was glowing
I had never imagined a body so loving
I had never imagined a body so golden

Early in the evening we had amazed one another
While the offices were closing
And couples grabbed at telephones
And all the lines were reaching
Early into evening
There was nothing much to do then
And nothing better either

Note from the Laboratory Assistant's Notebook

The Dodo came back.
It took off its hat. It took off its overcoat.
It took off its dark glasses and put them in its suit pocket.
It looked exhausted.

I made sure the doors were locked.
I turned off several lights.
I took the blood from the fridge
And injected it.

Next I sneaked into the back garden and buried
A manuscript containing
The History of Genetic Possibilities.
I washed my fingerprints from things.

I took a Bible down from the shelf.
Opening it at Genesis I sat waiting.
Outside, people not from the neighbourhood
Were asking questions.

The Complaint

'It will not last!'

'Who said that?' demanded the dragonfly,
Morning-blown, oblivious to sorrow.

'The best has passed!'

'Who blasphemed just then?'
Inquired the wren.

'All perishes!'

'How absurd,' said the gnat,
'What idiot believes that?'

All listened for an answer.
None came.

Night fell on Paradise,
Its children slept.
Hunched outside the Gates Adam wept.

A Few Questions about Adam

Who attended Adam's funeral?
Where was it held?
Was he cremated or buried?
Was Eve there?
Who else mourned him?
Did the serpent return to make amends?
Did it hang out at the back of the mourners,
Shuffling, a little embarrassed,
And what day of the week was it?
Was it a dull Wednesday afternoon?
Did Envy, disguised as Love,
Leak over the fading rim of Heaven,
Another infliction to set beside Knowledge?
Did it rain down in slow drips
On the befuddled mourners?
Did each drop of regret
Hiss on the hot fruit?
Would Adam, given time,
Have plucked it without
The serpent's interference?

The Mule's Favourite Dream

When the mule sings the birds will fall silent.
From among them they will choose a messenger.
It will fly to the court of the Emperor
And bowing with much decorum
Will complain bitterly.

And the Emperor, who had long ago banished all cages,
Who until that moment had been astonished
By the birds' flight and by their singing,
Will throw open the windows and listening
Will detect in the mule's song
Some flaw of which he is particularly fond,

And he will say to the bird, 'O stupid thing!
Let the mule sing,
For there has come about a need of change,
There is a hunger now, a need
For different things.'

This is the mule's favourite dream.
It's his own invention.
Deep in his brain's warren it blossoms.

You'd Better Believe Him

Discovered an old rocking-horse in Woolworth's,
He tried to feed it, but without much luck.
So he stroked it, had a long conversation about
The trees it came from, the attics it had visited.
Tried to take it out then
But the store detective he
Called the store manager who
Called the police who in court next morning said,
'He acted strangely when arrested,
His statement read simply "I believe in rocking-horses."
We have reason to believe him mad.'
'Quite so,' said the prosecution.
'Bring in the rocking-horse as evidence.'
'I'm afraid it escaped, sir,' said the store manager.
'Left a hoofprint as evidence
On the skull of the store detective.'
'Quite so,' said the prosecution, fearful
Of the neighing
Out in the corridor.

A Small Dragon

I've found a small dragon in the woodshed.
Think it must have come from deep inside a forest
because it's damp and green and leaves
are still reflecting in its eyes.

I fed it on many things, tried grass,
the roots of stars, hazelnut and dandelion,
but it stared up at me as if to say, I need
food you can't provide.

It made a nest among the coal,
not unlike a bird's but larger,
it is out of place here
and is quite silent.

If you believed in it I would come
hurrying to your house to let you share my wonder,
but I want instead to see
if you yourself will pass this way.

Brer Rabbit's Howler

Brer Rabbit goes to the ball dressed as a dandy.
He feels good this evening.
Magnanimous towards all creatures,
He cannot understand
Why the dancers shy away from him.
What social misdemeanour is it now
That they stiffen at?
He's eaten the lice.
He's washed off the stench of burrows.
The myxomatosis scabs are healed.
What's left to complain about?
He dances to whatever tune's available,
The fox trot, the tango;
His green suit becomes him,
In his lapel
The baby's foot looks charming.

Brer Rabbit's Revenge

So Brer Rabbit re-enters the burrow.
All day he's been in the world of fantasy,
but now below the drenched allotment
he is at home again.

Through the walls of his burrow rain leaks,
the tunnels turn liquid;
his fur mud-soaked he screams
his hatred of make-believe.

All day he's been bunnying about –
smiling benevolently with the toy shop dummies,
wandering through the nursery
all winsome and innocent.

Now that above ground the children sleep
cocooned in love for him
something drops away and sweetness
is no longer bearable.

Soon enough those children will grow old.
Brer Rabbit climbs into his shroud.
He waits to haunt them.

Blake's Purest Daughter

'All things pass,
Love and mankind is grass'
– Stevie Smith

Must she always walk with Death, must she?
I went out and asked the sky.
No, it said, no,
She'll do as I do, as I do.
I go on forever.

Must she always walk with Death, must she?
I went and asked the soil.
No, it said, no,
She'll do as I do, as I do.
I will nourish her forever.

Must she always walk with Death, must she?
I listened to the water.
No, it said, no.
She'll do as I do, as I do.
I will cleanse her forever.

Must she always walk with Death, must she?
No, said the fire,
She'll burn as I burn, as I burn.
She will be in brilliance forever.

O but I am not Death, said Death slyly,
I am only no longer living,
Only no longer knowing exorbitant grief.
Do not fear me, so many share me.

Stevie elemental
Free now of the personal,
Through sky and soil
And fire and water,
Swim on, Blake's purest daughter!

Going Back and Going On

Trying to get back before night hid the way
And the path through Sharpham Wood was lost
I still found time to stop, and stopping found
A different path shining through the undergrowth.
It was real enough –
A sun that had been too high to light
The underside of leaves had sunk,
And ground level rays had lit
The tiny roots of things just begun.
Just now begun!
To think on this halfway through what time is left!
Among the dead and glittering brambles on the path
The miracle is obstinate.
There is no 'going back', no wholly repeatable route,
No rearranging time or relationships,
No stopping skin from flaking like a salmon's flesh.
Yet no end of celebration need come about,
No need to say,
'Such and such a thing is done and gone',
The mistake is in the words, and going back
Is just another way of going on.

The Wrong Number

I

One night I went through the telephone book name by name.
I moved in alphabetical order through London
Plundering living rooms, basements, attics,
Brothels and embassies.
I phoned florists' shops and mortuaries,
Politicians and criminals with a flair for crime;
At midnight I phoned butchers and haunted them with strange bleatings.
I phoned prisons and zoos simultaneously,
I phoned eminent surgeons at exactly the wrong moment.
Before I was half-way through the phone book
My finger was numb and bloody.
Not satisfied with the answers I tried again.
Moving frantically from A to Z needing confirmation
That I was not alone
I phoned grand arsonists who lived in the suburbs
And rode bicycles made out of flames.
No doubt my calls disturbed people on their deathbeds,
Their death rattles drowned by the constant ringing of telephones!
No doubt the various angels who stood beside them
Thought me a complete nuisance.
I *was* a complete nuisance.
I worried jealous husbands to distraction
And put various Casanovas off their stroke
And woke couples drugged on love.

I kept the entire London telephone system busy,
Darting from phone booth to phone booth
The Metropolitan phone-squad always one call behind me.
I sallied forth dressed in loneliness and paranoia –

The Phantom Connection.
    Moving from shadow to shadow,
Rushing from phone booth to phone booth till finally
    I sought out a forgotten number and dialled it.
A voice crackling with despair answered.
    I recognized my own voice and had nothing to say to it.

II

So I studied telephones constantly.
I wrote great and learned papers on the meaning of
        telephones.
I wondered what the last dispatch rider thought
Galloping past the telephone wires, his body full of stale
        arrows.
I wondered what it would have been like
If Caesar had had a telephone.

I thought of nothing but telephones.
Night after night I invented numbers.
I placed trunk-calls to non-existent cities.
Jesus! I received so many weird replies.

I wondered if the dead would like a telephone.
Perhaps we should plant phones in graves so that the
        dead
Might hold endless conversations
Gulping in the warm earth.

Telegrams and telephones,
And not an ounce of flesh between them
Only so much pain.

I began to consider them my enemy.
I joined underground movements dedicated to their
overthrowal.
I vowed absurd vows,
I sacrificed daisies.
My hands were bloody with pollen.

I can imagine the night when waking from a nervous
sleep
You find the telephone has dragged itself up the stairs one
at a time
And sits mewing,
The electronic pet waiting for its bowl of words.

*

Hello! Hello!
It's the evening phone-in show!
You've an abscess on the heart?
A tumour on the soul?
You're sleepless with grief?
You're in pain, you feel insane?
Neglected? Rejected?
You feel like a freak,
You feel bleak?
Lost your wife last week?
You're alone? Dying on your own?
Cancer crawling up the spine?
Well, fine!
Don't worry, don't care.
I'm on the air!
I'm DJ Despair,
I reek of the right answers!

*

It is so far from the beginning of telephones.

I thought of how it felt to be connected for the first time,
To be fifteen and uncertain while her mother says: 'Hang
on.'
O the ecstasy of waiting for her to come down from her
young room and answer!
The pinkness of telephones and the fragrance of telephones
And the innocence and earnestness of telephones!
I'm sure those wires still cross paradise,
Still fresh in the crushed ice of Yes!

Nothing in that conversation has changed.
She is still bemused at his agony as he struggles with the
language of telephones.
O to be connected so!
Before shadows passed over the wires,
Before trivia weighed them down,
When they trilled like sparrows and their voices were
bright.

*

Where does God hide his telephone number?
No doubt the clergy have committed that number to
memory.
Kneeling in their celestial phone booths
They phone him late at night while the lambs are suffering.
For the telephone is hard to resist
For it brings joy and misery without distinction
For the telephone is blameless
For it is a blessing to the hypochondriac
Both 'Help' and 'No' are in the word telephone.

And would it have made much difference
If Faustus had had a telephone?
Whose number was on Marilyn Monroe's lips the last time
she felt too tired?

What went wrong?
I was listening to the grave gossip.
Terror leaked from the mouth's pit.

In telephone exchanges the world over
The numbers are dying,
Vast morgues where the operators sleep-walk among the
babble,
Where the ghost phones lament
For all the calls that went wrong.

Death owns everyone's telephone number.

And the night?
How many telephone numbers does the night possess?
The night has as many telephone numbers as stars.

Staring at the Crowd

I saw the skeleton in everyone
And noticed how it walked in them,
And some, unconscious that Grinning Jack
Abided his time inside their flesh
Stared back, and wondered what I saw.
A boil on a face, the way they dressed,
Their vanities were small and obvious –
Women wore their coldest masks and men
Looked elsewhere and thought perhaps
I was some friend they'd dropped.
But I did not know them well enough to say
It's Grinning Jack I see today,
Not your beauty or your ugliness,
Nor how fresh you seem, nor how obvious
The chemical decay,
But the skeleton that every man
Ignores as calmly as he can,
Who'll kiss us on the cheek and blow
The floss of temporal things away.
It's Grinning Jack I see today,
And once seen he'll never go away.

Old Ladies in the Churchyard

At last I understand religion's sway
Over the poor crowd,
The frightened counting bead by bead
All their lonely follies;
Frail ladies wandering at light's edge
Believing in a place where spring
And its mass of blossom waits
Behind a gate pain cannot enter.
It's not called Paradise by them, but Heaven –
God's vast dose of valium that makes
their terror possible.

And all their fuzzy notions of that place
Rise, lark-pure, above my reasoning,
And sometimes I want to join them there
In that special atmosphere
Where sense is made of all despair.

At the grave's edge this evening the snowdrops
– Those little ballerinas shivering in the grey soil –
Have forgotten what dying was and are back again,
Without memory of frost,
With no notion of pain.

I bend to touch them. The carcass creaks,
A rook's nest of bone and tissue in which
The soul sways, and is blown by doubt,
And unlike those frail ladies
Can work nothing out.

The Choice

If I could choose the hour in which
Death chooses me
And the way in which
It will make its arbitrary choice

I can think of nothing better
Than to fall asleep near midnight
In a boat as it enters a new port,
In a boat with a clarity of stars
Above and below it;

And all around me
Bright music and voices
Laughing in a language
Not known to me.

I'd like to go that way,
Tired and glad,
With all my future before me,
Hungry still
For the fat and visible globe.

Drunk

An interpretation of Baudelaire's prose poem,
'The Drunken Song'

People are sober as cemetery stones!
They should be drunk, we should all be drunk!
Look, it's nearly night time and the sober news
Comes dribbling out of television sets –
It should be drunken news,
If only it were drunken news!
Only festivals to report and the sombre death
Of one ancient daisy.

It's time to get drunk, surely it's time?
Little else matters;
Sober the years twist you up,
Sober the days crawl by ugly and hunched and your soul –
It becomes like a stick insect!

I've spent so much time in the company
Of sober and respectable men,
And I learned how each sober thought is an obstacle laid
Between us and our longings.
We need to wash their words away,
We need to be drunk, to dance in the certainty
That drunkenness is right.

So come on, let's get drunk.
Let's get drunk on songs, on sex, on dancing,
On tulip juice or meditations,
It doesn't matter what –
But no soberness, not that!
It's obscene!

When everything you deluded yourself you wanted has gone
You can get drunk on the loss,
When you've rid yourself of the need for those things back
Then you will be light, you will be truly drunk.
For everything not tied down is drunk –
Boats and balloons, aeroplanes and stars –
All drunk.
And the morning steams with hangovers,
And the clouds are giddy
And beneath them swallows swoop, drunk,
And flowers stagger about on their stems
Drunk on the wind.

Everything in Heaven's too drunk to remember Hell.

And the best monsters are drunken monsters,
Trembling and dreaming of beanstalks
Too high for sober Jack to climb;
And the best tightrope walkers are drunken tightrope walkers,
A bottle in each hand they stagger above the net made
Of the audience's wish for them to fall.

Drunk, I've navigated my way home by the blurry stars,
I've been drunk on the future's possibilities
And drunk on its certainties,
And on all its improbabilities I've been so drunk
That logic finally surrendered.
And if one night of oblivion can wash away
All the petty heartache, then fine,
Reach for that ancient medicine.

And if you wake from drunkenness
Don't think too much about it,
Don't stop to think.

Don't bother asking clocks what time it is,
Don't bother asking anything that escapes from time
What time it is,
For it will tell you as it runs, leap-frogging over all
obstacles,
Why idiot, don't you know? It's time to get drunk!
Time not to be the prisoner of boredom or cemetery stones!
Be drunk on what you want,
Be drunk on anything, anything at all
But please –

Understand the true meaning of drunkenness!

The Last Gift

For Heinz Henghes

H.H. *'What's the story about?'*
B.P. *'About a mouse that gets eaten by an eagle.'*
H.H. *'Poor mouse.'*
B.P. *'No, the mouse becomes part of the eagle.'*
H.H. *'Lucky mouse. Perhaps I'll be that lucky.'*

Perhaps next time he will be
A musician playing in a hall in which
A few children fidget and dream
While the crowd regrets
What cannot help but pass.
Or perhaps he will be something a snowdrift's buried
And that's not found again,
Or the contradiction of blossom
On a stunted apple tree.

Perhaps, but all I know for certain
Is that already some friends are in their graves,
And for them the world is no longer fixed
In its stubborn details.
Astonished in moments of clarity to realize
How all that surrounds me has passed
Again and again through death,
I still strut without understanding
Between an entrance of skin and an exit of soil.

It is too much to expect he will come back
In the same form,
Molecule by sweet molecule reassembled.
When the grave pushes him back up
Into the blood or the tongue of a sparrow,
When he becomes the scent of foxglove,

Becomes fish or glow-worm,
When as a mole he nuzzles his way up
Eating worms that once budded inside him,
It's too much to expect that I'll still be around.

I'll not be here when he comes back
As a moth with no memory of flames.

It is a dubious honour getting to know the dead,
Knowing them on more intimate terms,
Friends who come and go in what at the last moment
Seems hardly a moment.
And now as one by dreamless one they are dropped
Into the never distant, dreamless grave,
As individual memory fades
And eye-bewildering light is put aside,
We grow baffled by the gift
Of the days that they are now denied.

Something Never Lost

There is a place where the raspberries burn
And the fat sparrows snore in peace;
Where apples have no fear of teeth,
And a tongue not used to dust
Sings of something never lost;
It is a place not far away.
It takes a lot of trust to reach,
And a spell only love can teach.

Whose Body Has Opened

Whose body has opened
Night after night
Harbouring loneliness,
Cancelling the doubts
Of which I am made,
Night after night
Taste me upon you.

Night and then again night,
And in your movements
The bed's shape is forgotten.
Sinking through it I follow,
Adrift on the taste of you.

I cannot speak clearly about you.
Night and then again night,
And after a night beside you
Night without you is barren.

I have never discovered
What alchemy makes
Your flesh different from the rest,
Nor why all that's commonplace
Comes to seem unique,

And though down my spine one answer leaks
It has no way to explain itself.

Song about Home

I have gone out, making a pathway through the morning,
Gone out, ankle-deep in silence,
Never to come back this way.
My brain wears a lining of frost, it sparkles,
My way is clear enough.

Call memory forest, and all the things that ever stunned
The roots of that forest,
Fed by voices so previous
The rain cannot shake them out, nor seasons cancel.
The stars are alive in me,
They go about like drunken satellites.

I'm obsessed, and the obsessions gladden.
I have gone to where the ant goes,
To where the bird whistles.
I follow the vast pathway a snail makes,
Drift unaware through the white dandelions.

Through negligence most friendships have faded,
But what does it matter?
There was never one place I belonged in.
I sing of how home is the place not yet visited,
Built out of longings, mapped out by accidents.

One Reason for Sympathy

I rescued a bee from a web last night.
It had been there several hours,
Numbed by the cold it could hardly fight
A spider half its size, one programmed
To string a web across the fattest flowers
And transform the pollen into bait.
My sympathy I know now was misplaced,
For it had found the right time in which to die.
I saved it while light sank into grass
And trees swelled to claim their space;
I saved it in a time of surface peace.
Next morning as I watched the broken web gather light
Seeing it ruined in the grass I understood
That I had done more harm than good,
And I felt confused by that act
Of egocentric tenderness.
I called it love at first, then care,
Then simple curiosity,
But there was a starker reason for such sympathy.
It is that one day I too will be caught out in the cold,
And finding terror in there being no help at hand
Will remember how once I tried to save a bee –
And hope the same is done for me.

The Bee's Last Journey to the Rose

I came first through the warm grass
Humming with spring,
And now swim through the evening's
Soft sunlight gone cold.
I'm old in this green ocean,
Going a final time to the rose.

North wind, until I reach it
Keep your icy breath away
That changes pollen into dust.
Let me be drunk on this scent a final time,
Then blow if you must.

Road Song

This evening at least I do not care
where the journey will be ending;
only a landscape softened now
by song and slow rainfall fills me.

The rest of things, her body crushed
against the whitest pillows, regrets
and the more concrete failures
are exiled and done with.

There is nowhere specially to get to.
The towns are identical, each one passed
takes deeper into evening
what sorrows I've brought with me.

In my head some voice is singing
a song that once linked us;
it has ceased to be of importance;
another song might replace it.

Now only my gawky shadow occupies
these roads going nowhere,
that by small towns are linked
and that by the darkness are cancelled.

Advice from the Original Gatecrasher

If you arrive outside Paradise and find
Entrance is by invitation only, and that anyway
From the ledger your name is missing,
Do not despair.
At the back of Paradise
In the huge wall that surrounds that place
There's a small door.
God and all his angels have forgotten it.
If something goes wrong and Heaven ignores you,
If what you are is paraded before you and mocked,
Do not despair; you have got too near
For your schemes to be abandoned.
If you are told to go away, to Hell,
To the blankness already experienced,
You simply sneak round the wall
To the small door at the back of Heaven,
You give it a bit of a push
And wriggling like a snake you squeeze yourself in.
And if you ever get hungry
No doubt somewhere you will find an apple tree,
And fruit to share quite generously.

Into My Mirror Has Walked

Into my mirror has walked
A woman who will not talk
Of love or of its subsidiaries,
But who stands there,
Pleased by her own silence.
The weather has worn into her
All seasons known to me,
In one breast she holds
Evidence of forests,
In the other, of seas.

I will ask her nothing yet
Would ask so much
If she gave a sign –

Her shape is common enough,
Enough shape to love.
But what keeps me here
Is what glows beyond her.

I think at times
A boy's body
Would be as easy
To read light into,
I think sometimes
My own might do.

Burning Genius

He fell in love with a lady violinist,
It was absurd the lengths he went to to win her affection.
He gave up his job in the Civil Service.
He followed her from concert hall to concert hall,
bought every available biography of Beethoven,
learnt German fluently,
brooded over the exact nature of inhuman suffering,
but all to no avail –

Day and night she sat in her attic room,
she sat playing her violin day and night,
oblivious of him,
and of even the sparrows that perched on her skylight
mistaking her music for food.

To impress her, he began to study music in earnest.
Soon he was dismissing Vivaldi and praising Wagner.
He wrote concertos in his spare time,
wrote operas about doomed astronauts and about monsters
who,
when kissed,
became even more furious and ugly.
He wrote eight symphonies taking care to leave several
unfinished,

It was exhausting.
And he found no time to return to that attic room.

In fact, he grew old and utterly famous.

And when asked to what he owed
his burning genius,
he shrugged and said little,

but his mind gaped back until he saw before him
the image of a tiny room,
in which a girl, hardly more than a child,
sat playing very badly a stammering violin
and perched on the skylight
the timid skeletons of sparrows still listened on.

Sometimes It Happens

And sometimes it happens that you are friends and then
You are not friends,
And friendship has passed.
And whole days are lost and among them
A fountain empties itself.

And sometimes it happens that you are loved and then
You are not loved,
And love is past.
And whole days are lost and among them
A fountain empties itself into the grass.

And sometimes you want to speak to her and then
You do not want to speak,
Then the opportunity has passed.
Your dreams flare up, they suddenly vanish.

And also it happens that there is nowhere to go and then
There is somewhere to go,
Then you have bypassed.
And the years flare up and are gone,
Quicker than a minute.

So you have nothing.
You wonder if these things matter and then
As soon as you begin to wonder if these things matter
That's when they begin to cease to matter
And caring is past,
And a fountain empties itself into the grass.

I Caught a Train that Passed the Town where You Lived

I caught a train that passed the town where you lived.
On the journey I thought of you.
One evening when the park was soaking
You hid beneath trees, and all round you dimmed itself
As if the earth were lit by gaslight.
We had faith that love would last forever.

I caught a train that passed the town where you lived.

A Children's Dozen

Geography Lesson

Our teacher told us one day he would leave
And sail across a warm blue sea
To places he had only known from maps,
And all his life had longed to be.

The house he lived in was narrow and grey
But in his mind's eye he could see
Sweet-scented jasmine clinging to the walls,
And green leaves burning on an orange tree.

He spoke of the lands he longed to visit,
Where it was never drab or cold.
I couldn't understand why he never left,
And shook off the school's stranglehold.

Then halfway through his final term
He took ill and never returned.
He never got to that place on the map
Where the green leaves of the orange trees burned.

The maps were redrawn on the classroom wall;
His name was forgotten, it faded away.
But a lesson he never knew he taught
Is with me to this day.

I travel to where the green leaves burn,
To where the ocean's glass-clear and blue,
To places our teacher taught me to love –
And which he never knew.

Mr Ifonly

Mr Ifonly
Sat down and he sighed,
'I could have done more,
If only I'd tried.

'If only I'd followed
My true intent,
If only I'd said
the things that I meant.

'If only I'd gone
And not stayed at home,
If only I'd taken
The chance to roam.

'If only I'd done
As much as I could,
And not simply done
The things that I should.

'If only a day
Had lasted a year,
If only I'd lived
Without constant fear.

'Now life's passed me by
And it's such a crime,'
Said Mr Ifonly,
Who'd run out of time.

A Boat in the Snow

On to the ocean's cold dark skin
Snowflakes are falling and are melting away.
How strange the snow seems out here!
How quickly the white blizzard is swallowed up by the
  waves.
Without the framework of land,
Each flake's transformed.
Like a trillion ocean-borne moths
They flick into existence, then go.
As the sky above and around me
Glitters with frosty flecks of stars,
So the deck of the boat glitters,
And I wonder, are whales sleeping
Out there in the world's depths, beyond
The boat's bow? And I wonder,
Do they really sleep? And how?
There is no one to ask.
Snuggled up in cabins
Passengers are dreaming,
And all round us still the snow is falling,
And the ship's deck has become
A moonlit field, a field adrift
On the dark skin of the world.
I would love to sail forever between islands of snow.

Hide-away Sam

Hide-away Sam sat in the darkness,
Pale as the day he was born,
A miser who stored up his blessings
Yet looked on blessings with scorn.

He peeked through a chink in the doorway,
A crack on which the sun shone.
All the things he had craved danced past him,
He blinked, and they were gone.

A ladder was stretched up to Heaven,
Its rungs were covered in dew,
At its foot was a bucket of diamonds
(From the sky God had stolen a few)

And beyond the ladder an orchard
Where bees dunked in pollen flew
Between the falling blossom
And the core of a fruit that was new.

'Time to come out and enjoy life!'
A voice boomed down from above.
'Time to swap ten aeons of darkness
For one bright second of love.'

But Hide-away Sam shrank inwards.
He refused to open the door.
The Angel of Mercy lost patience,
Shrugged, and said no more.

The Apple-flavoured Worm

When the rivers were pregnant with fishes
And the trees were pregnant with buds,
When the earth was fat with seeds
And a million other goods,
Taking a snooze in an apple
Was an apple-flavoured worm.
It heard God's voice say, 'Bite.
Eve, it is your turn.'

When the sky was bluer than blue
And the earth shone bright as a pin,
Before Paradise has been abandoned
Or a tongue had invented a sin,
Taking a snooze in an apple
Was the apple-flavoured worm.
It heard God's voice say, 'Bite.
Adam, it's now your turn.'

Then the bloom was gone from the garden,
The first petal had dropped from a flower,
The wound in the rib's cage was healed
And Satan had lived for an hour.
And wide awake in the apple
The apple-flavoured worm
Heard the Gates of Heaven closing
And a key of iron turn.

A Poet I Know

I know a poet whose poems
Were told to shut up and wait.
They were impatient poems.

I know a poet whose poems
Hated everything.
They were lonely poems.

I know a poet whose poems
Were fed on blood.
They were angry poems.

I know a poet whose poems
Lived on thin air.
They were empty poems.

I know a poet whose poems
Were fed to him on a spoon.
They were lazy poems.

I know a poet whose poems
Told the best jokes in the world.
They were popular poems.

I know a poet whose poems
Lived on laughter and sunshine.
They were glorious poems.

I know a poet whose poems
Were the richest poems in the world.
They kept falling through the holes in his pockets.

Tiger Shadows

I wish I was a tiger in the Indian jungle
The jungle would be my teacher

No school
And the night sky a blackboard smudged with stars
I wish I was a tiger in the Indian jungle

Kitten-curious
I'd pad about on paws big as frying pans

While the monkeys chatted in the trees above me
I'd sniff the damp jungly air
Out of exotic flowers I would make a crown of pollen

If I were a tiger in the Indian jungle
My eyes would glitter among the dark green leaves
My tail would twitch like a snake

I would discover abandoned cities
Where no human feet had trod for centuries

I would be lord of a lost civilization
And leap among the vine-covered ruins

I wish I was a tiger in the Indian jungle
As the evening fell
I'd hum quiet tiger-tunes to which the fireflies would dance

I'd watch the red, bubbling sun
Go fishing with its net of shadows

While the hunters looked for me miles and miles away
I'd lie stretched out in my secret den

I would doze in the strawberry-coloured light
Under the golden stripy shadows of the trees
I would dream a tiger's dream

In Tintagel Graveyard

In an ancient cemetery overlooking the sea, I saw fresh flowers that had been placed on the grave of a boy who had drowned more than a century ago.

Who brought flowers to this grave?
'I,' said the wren.
'I brought them as seeds and then
Watched them grow.'

'No,' said the wind. 'That's not true.
I blew them across the moor and sea,
I blew them up to the grave's door.
They were a gift from me.'

'They came of their own accord,'
Said the celandine.
'I know best. They're brothers of mine.'

'I am Death's friend,'
Said the crow. 'I ought to know.
I dropped them into the shadow of the leaning stone.
I brought the flowers.'

'No,' said Love,
'It was I who brought them,

'With the help of the wren's wing,
With the help of the wind's breath,
With the help of the celandine and the crow.

'It was I who brought them
For the living and the dead to share,
I was the force that put those flowers there.'

The Boy Who Broke Things

The boy kept breaking things.
He broke the one window through which the world looked bright.
He broke bottles.
He broke promises.
He broke his mother's heart.
He broke the lock on the cupboard in which she kept the sky,
And so she floated off,
And was lost amongst clouds forever.
He broke the lock on the box in which his father kept the ocean.
His father was swept away and drowned,
And the boy never saw him again.
Angry, he stomped on the earth and tried to break it,
But it was a tough nut, the earth –
Far tougher than him.
And his anger grew,
Until it became a tree inside him,
And all its leaves were poisonous, and nothing sang,
And all its branches were empty.
The boy was angry.
He tore the curtain that separated life from death,
And so he could no longer tell
What was living and what was dead inside him.
He smashed the clues we use to separate fact from fiction,
So they became one thing to him.
His anger was like a nasty giant.
He was angry, but he could not say why
The answer to his anger stuck in his throat.
It was a secret he did not want to keep, but could not get rid of.
And the bottled-up pain inside him was like a mad genie,
And he wept and he wept and he wept.

Insects in the Stable

From The Dittisham Nativity

Who saw the birth,
When holy blood flowed,
Red as a rose?
I did, said the spider,
But nobody knows.
I sat in the corner and saw Christ born.
How sweet that morn!
I too, said the fly,
I saw the birth
With my multiple eye,
I saw Christ born.
And I hummed above him,
Said the bee,
How sweet he seemed to me.
And I,
Said the beetle,
I peered out
From under a nettle
Tall as a steeple.
I saw Christ born
That sweet morn!
And I was the first to drink his blood,
Said the mosquito,
Shunned from that day forth,
How was I to know?
I'm not to blame.
And I flew towards his light
As towards a flame,
Said the moth,
I snuggled down
And chomped upon his swaddling cloth.

Reading the Classics

The Secret Garden will never age.
The tangled undergrowth remains as fresh
As when the author put down her pen.
Its mysteries are as poignant now as then.

On the track the Railway Children wait;
Alice still goes back and forth through the glass;
In Tom's Midnight Garden Time unfurls
And children still discover secret worlds.

At the Gates of Dawn Pan plays his pipes;
Mole and Ratty still float in awe downstream.
The weasels watch, hidden in the grass.
None care how quickly human years pass.

Though Time's a thief it cannot thieve
One page from the world of make-believe.

The Bird Table

Grandad's old bird table
Dragged more birds down out the sky
Than a cat ever dreamed of.
I try to conjure up how it looked when new,
But fail, and see only an upright pole, the broken table
Dangling ghost-pale in a corner.
Abandoned now beneath the green dust of a birch tree
It seems so old and useless.
Yet once it reached up,
Exulting in a feast of crumbs,
Its wooden palm open to heaven.
If birds had a sense of history,
What would they make of it?
A sacrificial altar elbowed aside by time?
A monolith supporting the legend of how once
There was a world of plenty?
A time when Bird and Man
Lived in harmony,
Spoke one tongue, exchanged gifts.
Song for bread. Bread for song.

The Tragedy

Behind the cooker yesterday
I found a pencil-written note.
It had been there some years,
Brooding and awaiting its moment
Among the chip-fat and ketchup.

'Bastard,' it read,
'I'll not be back again.
It's after midnight. This time
I'm going forever.'

It was from someone whose name
I could not decipher.
Grease had obscured the signature.

I was not even sure whether
It was addressed to me.
Perhaps. Perhaps not.
I neither knew nor cared.

That is the tragedy.

January Gladsong

Seeing as yet nothing is really well enough arranged
the dragonfly will not yet sing
nor will the guests ever arrive
quite as naked as the tulips intended.
Still, because once again I am wholly glad of living,
I will make all that is possible step out of time
to a land of giant hurrays! where the happy monsters dance
and stomp darkness down.

Because joy and sorrow must finally unite and the small
heart-
beat of sparrow be heard above jet-roar, I will sing
not of tomorrow's impossible paradise
but of what now radiates.
Forever the wind is blowing the white clouds in someone's
pure direction;

In all our time birdsong has teemed and couples known
that darkness is not forever,
In the glad boat we sail the gentle and invisible ocean
where none have ever really drowned.

Hair Today, No Her Tomorrow

'I've been upstairs,' she said.
'Oh yes?' I said.
'I found a hair,' she said.
'A hair?' I said.
'In the bed,' she said.
'From a head?' I said.
'It's not mine,' she said.
'Was it black?' I said.
'It was,' she said.
'I'll explain,' I said.
'You swine,' she said.
'Not quite,' I said.
'I'm going,' she said.
'Please don't,' I said.
'I hate you!' she said.
'You do?' I said.
'Of course,' she said.
'But why?' I said.
'That black hair,' she said.
'A pity,' I said.
'Time for truth,' she said.
'For confessions?' I said.
'Me too,' she said.
'You what?' I said.
'Someone else,' she said.
'Oh dear,' I said.
'So there!' she said.
'Ah well,' I said.
'Guess who?' she said.
'Don't say,' I said.
'I will,' she said.
'You would,' I said.
'Your friend,' she said.
'Oh damn,' I said.
'And his friend,' she said.

'Him too?' I said.
'And the rest,' she said.
'Good God,' I said.

'What's that?' she said.
'What's what?' I said.
'That noise?' she said.
'Upstairs?' I said.
'Yes,' she said.
'The new cat,' I said.
'A cat?' she said.
'It's black,' I said.
'Black?' she said.
'Long-haired,' I said.
'Oh no,' she said.
'Oh yes,' I said.
'Oh shit!' she said.
'Goodbye,' I said.

'I lied,' she said.
'You lied?' I said.
'Of course,' she said.
'About my friend?' I said.
'Y-ess,' she said.
'And the others?' I said.
'Ugh,' she said.
'How odd,' I said.
'I'm forgiven?' she said.
'Of course,' I said.
'I'll stay?' she said.
'Please don't,' I said.
'But why?' she said.
'I lied,' I said.
'About what?' she said.
'The new cat,' I said.
'It's white,' I said.

The Cynic's Only Love Poem

Love comes and goes
And often it has paused,
Then comes back to see
The damage it has caused.

Dress Senseless

Ah, the futility of it!
Spending so much time in front of mirrors
When the soul itself is threadbare!

I Tried to Find My Voice

I tried to find my voice, a voice lost
In a night thickened by paranoia,
In a night crowded out by doubts
It could not articulate.
I had let go of it through negligence,
As at a carnival one lets go a child's hand.

I rummaged through a jumble sale of bodies,
Listened to advice devoid of meaning;
My voice was like a moth, its few colours
Worn to exhaustion.
It was drunk and lost, it was battered
And flung everywhere.

I tried to find it in the beds
Of solemn girls disguised as women,
I tried to find it among the men I envied.
I searched for it among its own inventions.

I had arranged my life around that voice,
Absurdly relied on it to explain
Who and what I was, as if either mattered.
In strange towns I used it to advantage.
Whatever it could fish out from the night
I accepted.

No matter; it was the one voice I let delude me.
Maybe it was getting the better of me,
Maybe it was envious and screamed at times,
Certainly it said things of which I'd grown ashamed
But I forgave it its blindness and tantrums
Hoping it would change.

And now it is beyond change.
My mouth cannot find it.
I have lost it; and no longer wish it back.
In winter I will make a voice out of snow,
In spring I will make a voice out of flowers,
In summer and autumn I will make a voice
With what is at hand.

The complaints it carried like credentials are misplaced
And its mouthful of reasons are blown away,
And its mouthful of tragedies
Have become light as dandelion seeds.

Angel Wings

In the morning I opened the cupboard
and found inside it a pair of wings,
a pair of angel's wings.
I was not naive enough to believe them real.
I wondered who had left them there.

I took them out the cupboard,
brought them over to the light by the window
and examined them.
You sat in the bed in the light by the window grinning.

'They are mine,' you said.
You said that when we met
you'd left them there.

I thought you were crazy.
Your joke embarrassed me.
Nowadays even the mention of the word angel
embarrasses me.

I looked to see how you'd stuck the wings together.
Looking for glue, I plucked out the feathers.
One by one I plucked them till the bed was littered.

'They are real,' you insisted,
your smile vanishing.

And on the pillow your face grew paler.
Your hands reached to stop me but
for some time now I have been embarrassed by the word
   angel,
For some time in polite or conservative company
I have checked myself from believing

anything so untouched and yet so touchable
had a chance of existing.

I plucked them
till your face grew even paler;
intent on proving them false
I plucked
and your body grew thinner.
I plucked till you all but vanished.

Soon beside me in the light,
beside the bed in which you were lying
was a mass of torn feathers;
glueless, unstitched, brilliant,
reminiscent of some vague disaster.

In the evening I go out alone now.
You say you can no longer join me.
You say
without wings it is not possible.
You say
ignorance has ruined us,
disbelief has slaughtered.

You stay at home,
listening on the radio
to sad and peculiar music,
you who fed on belief,
who fed on the light I'd stolen.

Next morning when I opened the cupboard
out stepped a creature,
blank, dull, and too briefly sensual
it brushed out the feathers gloating.
I must review my disbelief in angels.

The Stolen Orange

When I went out I stole an orange
I kept it in my pocket
It felt like a warm planet

Everywhere I went smelt of oranges
Whenever I got into an awkward situation
I'd take the orange out and smell it

And immediately on even dead branches I saw
The lovely and fierce orange blossom
That smells so much of joy

When I went out I stole an orange
It was a safeguard against imagining
There was nothing bright or special in the world

A Blade of Grass

You ask for a poem.
I offer you a blade of grass.
You say it is not good enough.
You ask for a poem.

I say this blade of grass will do.
It has dressed itself in frost,
It is more immediate
Than any image of my making.

You say it is not a poem,
It is a blade of grass and grass
Is not quite good enough.
I offer you a blade of grass.

You are indignant.
You say it is too easy to offer grass.
It is absurd.
Anyone can offer a blade of grass.

You ask for a poem.
And so I write you a tragedy about
How a blade of grass
Becomes more and more difficult to offer,

And about how as you grow older
A blade of grass
Becomes more difficult to accept.

Meat

Some pretty little thoughts,
some wise little songs,
some neatly packed observations,
some descriptions of peacocks, of sunsets,
some fat little tears,
something to hold to chubby breasts,
something to put down,
something to sigh about,
I don't want to give you these things.
I want to give you meat,
the splendid meat,
the blemished meat.
Say, here it is,
here is the active ingredient,
the thing that bothers history,
that bothers priest and financier.
Here is the meat.

The sirens wailing on police cars,
the ambulances alert with pain,
the bricks falling on the young
queens in night parks
demand meat,
the real thing.

I want to give you something
that bleeds as it leaves my hand
and enters yours,
something that by its rawness,
that by its bleeding
demands to be called real.

In the morning, when you wake,
the sheets are blood-soaked.
For no apparent reason
they're soaked in blood.
Here is the evidence you have been waiting for.
Here is the minor revelation.

A fly made out of meat lands
on a wall made out of meat.
There is meat in the pillows we lie on.
The eiderdowns are full of meat.
I want to give it you,
share the headache of the doctor
bending irritated by the beds
as he deals out the hushed truth about the meat,
the meat that can't be saved,
that's got to end,
that's going to be tossed away.

At night the meat rocks between sheets
butchered by its longings.

You can strip the meat,
you can caress and have sex with it –
the thing that carries its pain around,
that's born in pain,
that lives in pain,
that eats itself to keep itself in pain.

My neighbours driving away in their cars
are moody and quiet and do not talk much.
I want to fill their cars with meat,
stuff it down their televisions,
I want to leave it in the laundromats
where the shy secretaries gather.

At the fashionable parties the fashionable meat dances,
studded with jewellery it dances.
How delicately it holds its wine glass,
How intelligently it discusses
the latest mass butchering.

Repetitive among the petals,
among the songs repetitive,
I want the stuff to breathe its name,
the artery to open up and whisper:
I am the meat,
the sole inventor of Paradise.
I am the thing denied entrance into Heaven,
awkward and perishable,
the most neglected of mammals.
I am the meat that glitters,
that weeps over its temporariness.

I want the furniture to turn into meat,
the door handle as you touch it
to change into meat.

The meat you are shy to take home to mother,
the meat you are,
gone fat and awkward.
Hang it above your bed.
In the morning when you wake drowsy
find it in the washbasin.
Nail it to the front door.
In the evening leave it out on the lawns.
The meat that thinks the stars are white flies.
Let the dawn traveller find it among hedgerows
waiting to offer itself as he passes.
Leave it out among the night patrols and the lovers.
Leave it between the memoranda of politicians.

Here is the active ingredient;
here is the thing that bothers history,
that bothers priest and financier.
Pimply and blunt and white,
it comes towards you with its arms outstretched.
You are in love with the meat.

Poem Written in the Street on a Rainy Evening

Everything I lost was found again.
I tasted wine in my mouth.
My heart was like a firefly; it moved
Through the darkest objects laughing.

There were enough reasons why this was happening
But I never stopped to think about them.
I could have said it was your face,
Could have said I'd drunk something idiotic,

But no one reason was sufficient,
No one reason was relevant;
My joy outshone
Dull surroundings.

A feast was spread; a world
Was suddenly made edible.
And there was forever to taste it.

Simple Lyric

When I think of her sparkling face
And of her body that rocked this way and that,
When I think of her laughter,
Her jubilance that filled me,
It's a wonder I'm not gone mad.

She is away and I cannot do what I want.
Other faces pale when I get close.
She is away and I cannot breathe her in.

The space her leaving has created
I have attempted to fill
With bodies that numbed upon touching,
Among them I expected her opposite,
And found only forgeries.

Her wholeness I know to be a fiction of my making,
Still I cannot dismiss the longing for her;
It is a craving for sensation new flesh
Cannot wholly calm or cancel,
It is perhaps for more than her.

At night above the parks the stars are swarming.
The streets are thick with nostalgia;
I move through senseless routine and insensitive chatter
As if her going did not matter.
She is away and I cannot breathe her in.
I am ill simply through wanting her.

Vanishing Trick

Your back is long and perfect, it is clear.
It moves away from me, it moves away, I watch it going.
In the morning I watch you gather up
longings mistakenly scattered.

I watch you gather up your face, your body,
watch till another creature walks about,
dressed and impatient.

You contained all there need be of love,
all there need be of jubilance and laughter you contained it.
And now you are its opposite,
you talk of going as if going were the smallest matter.

There do not have to be reasons for such changes,
there do not have to be.
In the morning bodies evaporate and nothing
can quite hold them together.

Suddenly everything changes.
Less than a second passes and nothing's the same.
Something that clung a moment ago lets go as if
all its clinging meant nothing.

Now in the bathroom the razors wait like a line of little
  friends,
they glow as much as roses,
they glow, glow with pain, with their own electricity,
they glow with darkness.

When you have gone they will turn their heads in my
direction.
Inquisitive and eager they will welcome me,
but I will not listen.
I will try your vanishing trick and manage,
I will manage to feel nothing.

The Sick Equation

In school I learned that one and one made two,
It could have been engraved in stone,
An absolute I could not question or refute.
But at home, sweet home, that sum was open to dispute –
In that raw cocoon of parental hate is where
I learned that one and one stayed one and one.
What's more, because all that household's anger and its
   pain
Stung more than any teacher's cane
I came to believe how it was best
That one remained one,
For by becoming two, one at least would suffer so.

Believing this I threw away so many gifts –
I never let love stay long enough to take root,
But thinking myself of too little worth
I crushed all its messengers.

I grew – or did not grow –
And kept my head down low,
And drifted with the crowd,
One among the many whose dreams of flight
Weighed down the soul,
And kept it down,
Because to the flightless
The dream of flight's an anguish.

I stayed apart, stayed one,
Claiming separateness was out of choice,
And at every wedding ceremony I saw
The shadow of that albatross – divorce –

Fall over groom and bride,
And I took small comfort in believing that, to some degree
They too still harboured dreams of flying free.

I was wrong of course,
Just as those who brought me up were wrong.
It's absurd to believe all others are as damaged as
ourselves,
And however late on, I am better off for knowing now
That given love, by taking love all can in time refute
The lesson that our parents taught,
And in their sick equation not stay caught.

Jesus Christ Was out Walking

Jesus Christ was out walking
Getting a bit of fresh air
When someone appeared before him
Holding a questionnaire.

There were only a couple of questions.
They were simple and clear.
Who is the God I should turn to?
And, Does he live down here?

In a nearby street the Protestants
Waved banners and banged on a drum.
Jesus watched them in horror,
And was suddenly struck dumb.

The poor Lord was in a quandary,
There were so many gods around.
High, Low, and Anglican
And a few that were underground.

Buried deep in the suburbs
In a Methodist church, God
Dressed pleasantly and conservatively
And frowned on anything odd.

And across the road the Christian Brothers
Knelt in a schoolroom and prayed
And found sin where none was intended
And daily had it flayed.

Above a bank the Mormons,
Unbending and odd,
Put money aside for the afterlife
And prayed to a penny-wise God.

Yet another God lived with the Jesuits
In a rich and beautiful place.
They all played chess with the Devil
And theologized with grace.

The God of the Trappists was silent.
The monks were all telepaths
In whose heads a million voices whispered,
As in a psychopath's.

Jesus Christ was out walking
Getting a bit of fresh air
When the Devil asked him a question
That filled him with despair.

The Critics' Chorus

'How he got to the point of thinking this sort
of thing was a poem is a good and appalling question . . .'
– Donald Davie

Of course they were right:
The poem lacked a certain tightness,
Its inventions were chaotic.

In the bleak farmhouse Rimbaud
remembering the jewelled spider webs,
The smoking pond, the banished sideshows.

Of course they were right:
The poems were not fit to be taken seriously,
Mere candyfloss, the efforts of a stablehand.

In Rome coughing up the rose-shaped phlegm
Keats taking the final opiate,
exiled among the fume of poppies.

Of course they were right:
He could have found all he wrote
In the dustbins he emptied.

Where's Hyatt now?
Still drinking the blind wind?
Ghost-junk still flowing in ghost-veins?

Of course they were right:
So much of what she wrote was doggerel,
Mere child's play.

In a London suburb Stevie,
Blake's grandchild,
fingering a rosary made of starlight.

Of course they were right:
In all the poems something went astray,
Something not quite at home in their world,
Something lost.

It was something to do with what the poem lacked
Saved it from oblivion,
A hunger nothing to do with the correct idiom
In which to express itself

But a need to eat a fruit far off
From the safe orchard,
Reached by no easy pathway
Or route already mapped.

Her Coldness Explained

She said no man had ever hurt her,
She, who beside me like a statue lay.
And she would have me believe her heart
Was cold, and like a statue made of clay.

What? What did she say?
No man had ever hurt her?
She is so wrong.
Through her dreams her father walks night-long.

No Taxis Available

It is absurd not knowing where to go.

You wear the streets like an overcoat.
Certain houses are friends, certain houses
Can no longer be visited.
Old love affairs lurk in doorways, behind windows
Women grow older. Neglection blossoms.

You have turned down numerous invitations,
Left the telephones unanswered, said 'No'
To the few that needed you.
Stranded on an island of your own invention
You have thrown out messages, longings.

How useless it is knowing that where you want to go
Is nowhere concrete.
The trains will not take you there,
The red buses glide past without stopping,

No taxis are available.

It Is Time to Tidy Up Your Life

It is time to tidy up your life!
Into your body has leaked this message.
No conscious actions, no broodings
Have brought the thought upon you.
It is time to take into account
What has gone and what has replaced it.
Living your life according to no plan
The decisions were numerous and
The ways to go were one.

You stand between trees this evening;
The cigarette in your cupped hand
Glows like a flower.
The drizzle falling seems
To wash away all ambition.
There are scattered through your life
Too many dreams to entirely gather.

Through the soaked leaves, the soaked grass,
The earth-scents and distant noises
This one thought is re-occurring:
It is time to take into account what has gone,
To cherish and replace it.
You learnt early enough that celebrations
Do not last forever,
So what use now the sorrows that mount up?

You must withdraw your love from that
Which would kill your love.
There is nothing flawless anywhere,
Nothing that has not the power to hurt.
As much as hate, tenderness is the weapon of one
Whose love is neither perfect nor complete.

The Package

At dinner, long-faced and miserable,
They cast sly glances at the other guests,
The pink-kneed husband and his wife
Sitting with their five-year-old, complaining pest.
The holiday brochure they'd believed in, lied,
Still they blamed each other for the clouds
And ever since arriving they had rowed.

After dinner, the child put to bed,
They bickered beneath the hotel's vine
And the ghosts of false what-might-have-beens
Surfaced with each extra glass of wine.
Theirs was a package holiday all right:
A package stuffed
With years of rootless longings and regrets.
Their bickering done, they sat mutely and both grieved
For what neither might have anyway achieved.

The next day they'd gone. They'd cut
Their holiday short, and carried back with them
A failure of another sort.
It was a failure to understand how all
Their arguments revolved around
An earlier package that they'd bought –
One promoted by both Church and State, one written
In the same tempting style; one over which
A watery sun had shone the same short while.

You Have Gone to Sleep

The nerves tense up and then:
You have gone to sleep.
Something not anchored in love drifts out of reach.
You have gone to sleep, or feign sleep,
It does not matter which.
Into the voice leaks bitterness.
The throat dries up, the tongue
Swells with complaints.
Once sleep was simply sleep.
The future stretched no further than
The pillow upon which your head was resting.
There were no awkward questions in the world,
No doubts caused love to fade
To a numbed kiss or howl,
Or caused trust to vanish.
You have gone to sleep.
A moment ago I found
Your mouth on mine was counterfeit.
Your sleep is full of exhaustions,
I cannot calm you,
There is no potion to wake you.
Do what I will, say what I will,
It is a sleep from which I am exiled.
You have gone to sleep,
A planet drifts out of reach.
If I spoke all night it would be no use,
You would not wake,
And silence, like words, you would no doubt
Mistake for ignorance.

So sleep. Across our window's small patch of Heaven
The stars like sheep are herded,
And like a satellite objective time
Circles calendars and mocks
The wounds we think are huge.
Sleep, don't be so tense.
There is no longer a need of barriers,
No need of dumb defence.
You are understood.
This night is the last on which there will be
Any kind of pretence.
Tomorrow something else might wake
What's gone to sleep.

Grim Comfort

Not knowing what they did, the dead
Taught me how best I should live
Out the days denied to them

As simply as the marigold
As simply as the weightless wren

They also taught me how
When I am become part of them

I will not miss the marigold
Or the weightless, singing wren

Perhaps

And when you turn your back something
That will not happen again happens,
And when you close your eyes perhaps
The stars rush about,
Or something changes colour.

And if you had been in a certain café,
In a certain street at a certain time,
Perhaps she would not have risen
And putting on a blue coat, vanished.

You hurry, and every place you pass
Pass places you have never been,
Where the future comes and goes,
Swirls round you and bypasses.

And all your dithering days you go
About the business of living,
Only for you it is not exactly living,
But filing away, ticking off, rearranging.

And nothing will ever be repeated again
Exactly as it happened,
And so much will have been missed
That has never been missed,
And yet still leaves you hungry and baffled.

And Nothing Is Ever as Perfect as You Want It to Be

You lose your love for her and then
It is her who is lost,
And then it is both who are lost,
And nothing is ever as perfect as you want it to be.

In a very ordinary world
A most extraordinary pain mingles with the small
  routines,
The loss seems huge and yet
Nothing can be pinned down or fully explained.

You are afraid.
If you found the perfect love
It would scald your hands,
Rip the skin from your nerves,
Cause havoc with a computed heart.

You lose your love for her and then it is her who is lost.
You tried not to hurt and yet
Everything you touched became a wound.
You tried to mend what cannot be mended,
You tried, neither foolish nor clumsy,
To rescue what cannot be rescued.

You failed,
And now she is elsewhere
And her night and your night
Are both utterly drained.

How easy it would be
If love could be brought home like a lost kitten
Or gathered in like strawberries,
How lovely it would be;
But nothing is ever as perfect as you want it to be.

Waves

And the one throwing the lifebelt,
Even he needs help at times,
Stranded on the beach,
Terrified of the waves.

On Reading an Acquaintance's Obituary

The other week it happened once again.
Another bit of me peeled off, revealing the bone.
It did not happen to me alone.
We who were once many are now one.
It is generations that die,
Individuals are the bits that flake away.

These Boys Have Never Really Grown into Men

These boys have never really grown into men,
despite their disguises, despite their adult ways,
their sophistication, the camouflage of their kindly smiles.
They are still up to their old tricks,
still at the wing-plucking stage. Only now
their prey answers to women's names.
And the girls, likewise, despite their disguises,
despite their adult ways, their camouflage of need,
still twist love till its failure seems not of their making.
Something grotesque migrates hourly
between our different needs,
and is in us all like a poison.
How strange I've not understood so clearly before
how liars and misers, the cruel and the arrogant
lie down and make love like all others,
how nothing is ever as expected, nothing is ever as stated.
Behind doors and windows nothing is ever as wanted.
The good have no monopoly on love.
All drink from it. All wear its absence like a shroud.

Interview with a Mythical Creature

Tell me about your paw?
My paw?
I see it is bleeding.
I trod on a nail.
Not a thorn? You didn't tread on a thorn from a rose
perhaps?
No, I trod on a nail. An old nail, dropped by Noah.
So you've been around a long time?
A century is only a day seen in a different light.
A different light?
A non-egocentric light.
Too true. Describe yourself for the benefit of our readers.
No.
No?
No, I wish to remain a mystery. A description would bog
down my essence.
But your paw . . .?
The one that bleeds or the one that burns?
The one that bleeds. You cannot remain a complete
mystery when we know you have a paw that bleeds.
If you knew absolutely nothing about me there would be
no mystery to begin with. The paw is an essential part of
the myth.
Tell me, what are you doing here?
Here?
In 21st-century London. Surely a myth would be more at
home in ancient Greece?
I am a very small myth. As you can see I am hardly larger
than a paw. I suit the times.

St Peter and the Devil

Peter stood outside the Gates of Heaven
With a far-away look in his eyes,
He was thinking of Rachel and Rebecca –
Of their scent and their plump brown thighs.

He stood outside the Gates of Heaven
Oiling the lock and testing the bars
When the Devil strolled up to greet him
With eyes that glittered like sulphurous stars.

The Devil spoke with the voice of Rebecca,
He came dressed in the body of Eve,
He snuggled up close to St Peter
And touched the old man on the sleeve.

'How well do you remember Rebecca?
Does sweet Rachel still heat up the blood?
Are they both as warm and as ripe
As the earth was after the Flood?'

'They're the same as ever,' said Peter,
He looked at the Devil and smiled,
'They're waiting for me behind the Gates.
You are the one who's exiled.'

The Right Mask

One night a poem came to a poet.
From now on, it said, you must wear a mask.
What kind of mask? asked the poet.
A rose mask, said the poem.
I've used it already, said the poet,
I've exhausted it.
Then wear the mask that's made
Out of the nightingale's song, use that mask.
But it's an old mask, said the poet,
It's all used up.
Nonsense! said the poem, it is the perfect mask.
Nevertheless, try on the God mask –
Now that mask illuminates Heaven.
But it is a tired mask, said the poet,
And the stars crawl about in it like ants.
Then try on the troubadour's mask, or the singer's mask,
Try on all the popular masks.
I have, said the poet, but they fit so awkwardly.
Now the poem was getting impatient,
It stamped its foot like a child. It screamed,
Then try on your own face!
Try on the one mask that terrifies you,
The mask no one else could possibly use,
The mask only you can wear out!
He tore at his face till it bled.
This mask? he asked, this mask?
Yes, said the poem, why not?
But he was tired of even that mask.
He had lived too long with it.
He tried to separate himself from it.
Its scream was muffled, it wept,
It tried to be lyrical.

It wriggled into his eyes and mouth,
Into his blood it wriggled.
The next day his friends did not recognize him,
The mask was utterly transparent.
Now it's the right mask, said the poem,
The right mask.
It clung to him lovingly
And never let go again.

April Morning Walk

So many of those girls I longed for are gone now,
Gone to ash that skin so inexpertly kissed,
Those stomachs I was hot for, gone beyond diaries into
  flames.
When the years tore up their surface beauty and threw it
  away
Like the bright wrappings on a parcel
What was left was what links all the breathing world,
An empathy,
The buried knowledge of our going.
It's so easy to forget how the years have poured away
And taken out of sequence and before their time
So many who deserved longer on this lush earth.

Along the streets in which I walked with them
The horse-chestnut leaves are opening like Chinese fans.
The dawn's clear light varnishes houses and gardens
And freezes forever under its glittering surface
So much half-remembered anguish.

A Cottage in the Lane, Dittisham

Whatever tragedies occurred in that house
Where finally she lived out her life alone,
No one knew or cared, least of all
Those who thought the place was theirs:
The squirrels nesting in the roof,
The mice in the cellar, and in the eaves
The birds that came each spring
And nested there, and sang
A song as pure as the rain-washed air.
How full her mind was, or how blank,
How rich she was or how poor
Was to them of no concern.
For all they knew the house was theirs,
So quietly had she lived in one small room.
An electric fire, a lamp,
And no desire to be elsewhere.
Now that the ghost-in-waiting she became
Has finally evaporated into the air,
The *For Sale* board's gone up,
A flag of surrender nailed against the cottage wall.
And the squirrels, the mice, the birds,
And all the rest who thought the place was theirs
Will soon move on. It's either that or else
Be caught in a pest-controller's snare.
Change is in the air.
Rich, green-wellied weekenders
Prowl through the undergrowth where once
A dynasty of toads held court.
The place will soon be bought.

In a Garden at the River's Edge

We drift out of fashion.
The pages of our early books
Grow yellow at the edges,
Time muffles their rawness.
Still, all's as it should be –
Real freedom lies in not caring
To make an impression,
To have no need to crouch
At the ego's dying furnace
Blowing on small embers.
Longings change,
Ambition melts like ice,
And letting go of what one was
Need be no sacrifice.

*

It's evening. Nostalgia threatens:
Memory takes up residence in the bones,
Subsumes all else to its addictions.
From the closed-up soul it takes
The things that made it shine the best,
Then lets go the rest.

Now in a garden at the river's edge
I sit and watch the greenness go,
Watch the hollows fill with snow and write,
Almost as an afterthought, an epitaph:
So much of what I am is long ago.
I do not mind that it is so.

Cinders

You never went to a ball, ever.
In all your years sweeping kitchens
No fairy godmother appeared, never.

Poor, poor sweetheart,
This rough white cloth, fresh from the hospital laundry,
Is the only theatre gown you've ever worn.

No make-up. Hair matted with sweat.
The drip beside your bed discontinued.
Life was never a fairy tale.

Cinders soon.

The Betrayal

By the time I got to where I had no intention of going
Half a lifetime had passed.
I'd sleepwalked so long. While I dozed
Houses outside which gas-lamps had spluttered
Were pulled down and replaced,
And my background was wiped from the face of the earth.

There was so much I ought to have recorded,
So many lives that have vanished –
Families, neighbours; people whose pockets
Were worn thin by hope. They were
The loose change history spent without caring.
Now they have become the air I breathe,
Not to have marked their passing seems such a betrayal.

Other things caught my attention:
A caterpillar climbing a tree in a playground,
A butterfly resting on a doorknob.
And my grandmother's hands!
Though I saw those poor, sleeping hands
Opening and closing like talons,
I did not see the grief they were grasping.
The seed of my long alienation from those I loved
Was wrapped in daydreams.

Something I've never been able to pinpoint
Led me away from the blood I ought to have recorded.
I search my history for reasons, for omens. But what use
  now
Zodiacs, or fabulous and complicated charts
Offered up by fly-brained astrologers?
What use now supplications?

In the clouds' entrails I constantly failed
To read the true nature of my betrayal.
What those who shaped me could not articulate
Still howls for recognition as a century closes,
And their homes are pulled down and replaced,
And their backgrounds are wiped from the face of the
earth.

Song of the Grateful Char

I'll scrub the doorstep till it blinds you,
I'll polish the candlesticks till they burn,
I'll crawl across the carpet
And suck up all your dirt,

Though the cast-off clothes you gave me
Are much too grand to wear
I'll don them in the bedroom,
And no doubt I'll weep there.

I'll wash the shit from your toilet,
The stiffness from your sheets.
Madam, thank you for employment.
Can I come again next week?

'Sweetheart,' said the banker's wife,
'I too know of despair,
I think about it often
In my house in Eaton Square.'

'Sweetheart,' said the doctor,
'I've no advice today.'
Pain had made him indifferent.
He turned his head away.

Among a pile of nightmares
I heard a woman scream.
'Hush,' said the psychiatrist,
'It is a common dream.'

There are many kinds of poverty,
My mother knew them well,
She sat and counted them in a tenement
A mile or so from Hell.

Ward Sixteen

At 2 a.m. last night, beyond the opaque doors of the hospital ward
in which I kept vigil, a glow appeared.
The duty nurse, bent over her reports, noticed nothing.
There was no sound other than the wheeze and creak of human wreckage,
of souls adrift in a drugged sleep, clinging still to bodies washed
by tidal waves of pain.

There was no other light
but the low-watted bulb on the nurse's table.
The ward door had not opened,
yet that glow entered,
pouring through the substance of the door
as if no barrier existed.

I thought it was my tiredness,
my own grief at an oncoming separation
that had caused a trick of light, a freak hallucination.
But the glow persisted. Drifting towards me
it flowed through the beds themselves,
and as it searched among the patients
it took shape, and I froze in awe.

It had become a creature, seven foot tall, hunched and radiant,
its golden skin the texture of a moth's wing.
It had come, breaking through the thin crust
that separates the mind from angels.

And by its light I saw how,
through the minute cracks in the surface of the hospital
walls,
the horror of dying like liquid spilt.

Unaware of me, as if it were I who was insubstantial,
it crouched beside the bed in which my mother was lying
and stretching out a hand towards her
brushed all the hours of her life aside.

Under thin lids her eyes moved,
And though from that befuddled cocoon in which physical
time was trapped
there came no final leavetaking,
something beyond doubt eased the terror
that came and went with each breath,
that came and went, then went,
and was gone forever.

How normal the ward seemed a moment later.
Beyond the opaque doors a solitary light-bulb glowed.
The duty nurse yawned, not in the least distracted.

The Armada

Long long ago
when everything I was told was believable
and the little I knew was less limited than now,
I stretched belly down on the grass beside a pond
and to the far bank launched a child's armada.
A broken fortress of twigs,
the paper-tissue sails of galleons,
the waterlogged branches of submarines –
all came to ruin and were on flame
in that dusk-red pond.
And you, mother, stood behind me,
impatient to be going,
old at twenty-three, alone,
thin overcoat flapping.
How closely the past shadows us.
In a hospital a mile or so from that pond
I kneel beside your bed and, closing my eyes,
reach out across the years to touch once more
that pond's cool surface,
and it is your cool skin I'm touching;
for as on a pond a child's paper boat
was blown out of reach
by the smallest gust of wind,
so too have you been blown out of reach
by the smallest whisper of death,
and a childhood memory is sharpened,
and the heart burns as that armada burnt,
long, long ago.

Inessential Things

What do cats remember of days?

They remember the ways in from the cold,
The warmest spot, the place of food.
They remember the places of pain, their enemies,
the irritation of birds, the warm fumes of the soil,
the usefulness of dust.
They remember the creak of a bed, the sound
of their owner's footsteps,
the taste of fish, the loveliness of cream.
Cats remember what is essential of days.
Letting all other memories go as of no worth
they sleep sounder than we,
whose hearts break remembering so many
inessential things.

So Many Different Lengths of Time

Cuanto vive el hombre por fin? Vive mil dias o uno solo?
Una semana o varios siglos? Por cuanto tiempo muere el hombre?
Que quiere decir 'para siempre'?
Preocupado per este asunto me dedique a aclarar las cosas.
– Pablo Neruda

How long is a man's life, finally?
Is it a thousand days, or only one?
One week, or a few centuries?
How long does a man's death last?
And what do we mean when we say, 'gone forever'?

Adrift in such preoccupations, we seek clarification.
We can go to the philosophers,
But they will grow weary of our questions.
We can go to the priests and the rabbis
But they might be too busy with administrations.

*

So, how long does a man live, finally?
And how much does he live while he lives?
We fret, and ask so many questions –
Then when it comes to us
The answer is so simple after all.

A man lives for as long as we carry him inside us,
For as long as we carry the harvest of his dreams,
For as long as we ourselves live,
Holding memories in common, a man lives.

His lover will carry his man's scent, his touch;
His children will carry the weight of his love.
One friend will carry his arguments,

Another will hum his favourite tunes,
Another will still share his terrors.

And the days will pass with baffled faces,
Then the weeks, then the months,
Then there will be a day when no question is asked,
And the knots of grief will loosen in the stomach,
And the puffed faces will calm.
And on that day he will not have ceased,
But will have ceased to be separated by death.
How long does a man live, finally?

A man lives so many different lengths of time.

Yes

Last night I dreamt again of Adam returning
To the Garden's scented, bubbling cauldron.

Eve was beside him,
Their shadows were cut adrift
And the hum of bees was in their blood,

And the world was slow and good and all
The warm and yawning newness of their flesh
Was fixed forever in the glow of 'Yes'.

Full Circle World

Good morning dear world,
So briefly known.
In flashes only seen,
So often missed
By eyes so self-obsessed.
Good morning dear earth,
With your clouds like flags unfurled
And your sun that walks on beams of frost
And lights all we thought lost.
Good morning dear mist,
Dear floating lakes of light through which
The numbed bee and its cargo sails.
Good morning dear sky,
Dear scented woven threads of air
That blow away despair
From this world so briefly known,
In flashes only seen,
So often missed
By eyes so self-obsessed.
Good morning dear world.

The Minister for Exams

When I was a child I sat an exam.
The test was so simple
There was no way I could fail.

Q1. Describe the taste of the moon.

It tastes like Creation, I wrote,
it has the flavour of starlight.

Q2. What colour is Love?

Love is the colour of the water a man
lost in the desert finds, I wrote.

Q3. Why do snowflakes melt?

I wrote, they melt because they fall
onto the warm tongue of God.

There were other questions.
They were as simple.

I described the grief of Adam when he was expelled from
  Eden.
I wrote down the exact weight of an elephant's dream.

Yet today, many years later,
for my living I sweep the streets
or clean out the toilets of the fat hotels.

Why? Because constantly I failed my exams.
Why? Well, let me set a test.

Q1. How large is a child's imagination?
Q2. How shallow is the soul of the Minister for Exams?

Tattoos

No doubt in her youth
The many tattoos on my grandmother's arms
Were bold and clear:
No grave-marks or burst blood vessels sullied
  the breast of the blue-bird that flew
    upwards from her wrist-bone;
On her biceps
The sails on the three-decked galleon were not yellow or
  wrinkled,
And each angry thorn on the blue-stemmed rose was
  needle-sharp,
Its folded petals unblurred by time.
A child, I studied those tattoos intently –
Back then they seemed as mysterious as runes to me.
But all those tribal decorations went the way of her own
  bravado.
Ageing, the colours faded,
And her world shrank to a small island in the brain,
A tumour on which memory was shipwrecked
Till finally that galleon came to rest
One fathom down beneath Liverpool clay,
Its sails deflated, the blue-bird mute,
The rose gone to seed.

Blindness

Pens in hand
People are furiously writing up their diaries
At the day's end –
How on earth can they know so soon
What has happened?

Creature Comforts

My creature comforts no longer comfort me.
Truth is, they never did.
It was always the thought
Of leaving them behind
Was the luxury.

Night Orchard

I've no idea what it is that's breeding
Beneath the sheet of corrugated tin
I left last year in the orchard's far corner.
Whatever it is, it keeps to itself. It shuffles about
Just beyond the corner of my eye.
I think it is best to leave things that way,
Neither of us knowing, or wanting to know,
What the other's up to.
It's late at night, and so calm you'd think
A truce had been called between species.
I sit on the moonlit bank and listen
To the orchard's other tenants move about.
Baby adders explore the tangled grass,
Rats roll apples that the wasps have spoiled
Down to their nests, badgers trundle
Along tribal paths. Things would be perfect
But for that patch of feral dark
That hides away, plotting the demise
Of all that is not itself. Whatever it is
It is something I must learn to accommodate,
A stain on the night that sooner or later
I must pluck up the courage to face, if not here
Then some other far less calm and lovely place.

There is a Boat down on the Quay

There is a boat down on the quay come home at last.
The paint's chipped, the sails stained as if
Time's pissed up against them.
I imagine the sea routes it's followed,
Sailing through the world's sunken veins
With its cargo of longings;
A little boat that's nuzzled its way
Into the armpits of forests,
That's sliced through the moon's reflection,
Through the phosphate that clings to the lips of waves.
I knew its crew once,
Those boys manacled to freedom
Who set sail over half a century ago,
And were like giants to me.
A solitary child in awe of oceans
I saw them peel their shadows from the land
And watched as they departed.

What did they think when they peered
Over the rim of the world,
Where Time roared and bubbled
And angels swooped like swallows?
Reading an ancient Morse code of starlight,
Stranded by the longing to be elsewhere,
What secrets did they learn to forget?
I longed to be among them,
A passenger curled up in fate's pocket,
I longed to be a part of them –
Those ghosts who set sail in my childhood,
Those phantoms who shaped me,
That marvellous crew for whom
I have stretched a simple goodbye
Out over a lifetime.

One Another's Light

I do not know what brought me here
Away from where I've hardly ever been and now
Am never likely to go again.

Faces are lost, and places passed
At which I could have stopped,
And stopping, been glad enough.

Some faces left a mark,
And I on them might have wrought
Some kind of charm or spell
To make their futures work,

But it's hard to guess
How one person on another
Works an influence.
We pass, and lit briefly by one another's light
Hope the way we go is right.